SIKHISM AT A GLANCE

GLIMPSES OF SIKH HISTORY (VOLUME 2)

BHUPENDER SINGH

RIGI PUBLICATION

SIKHISM AT A GLANCE

Glimpses of Sikh History (Volume 2)

BY

BHUPENDER SINGH

Originally published in India

ISBN: 978-93-95773-30-0

Published by RIGI PUBLICATION

777, Street no.9, Krishna Nagar

Khanna-141401 (Punjab), India

Website: www.rigipublication.com

Email: info@rigipublication.com

Phone: +91-9357710014, +91-9465468291

DEDICATION

This book is dedicated to the memory of those innumerable martyrs who, remained steadfast to their faith and made the supreme sacrifice during the dark period of persecution of the Sikhs (1606 – 1765) and in later times. It is also to remember and value the sacrifices that were made by these heroes and almost never acknowledged. And above all, the book is a special tribute, especially to the unknown and unsung brave martyrs whose sacrifices went unrecognized – you were as brave as the ones we honour today. For the freedom that we have today, they paid the awful cost. We tip our heads in respect and salute those brave hearts.

ACKNOWLEDGMENT

I am indebted to Dr Vinita Singh for reading the manuscript and making corrections and valuable suggestions and also for her immense support and assistance.

CONTENTS

PART ONE
IMPORTANT EVENTS
IN THE HISTORY OF THE SIKHS

PART TWO
NOTES

PREFACE

Bulky books with a large amount of information are no longer popular with the general public. What the present-day reader wants is the extract of all important aspects, submitted to them in the most simple, concise and lucid form. They have no time, patience or leisure to go into elaborate explanations and details. This is more so with the lay reader who is eager to discern a new subject. This book has been written, keeping their need in mind. The book gives a bird's eye-view of the history of the Sikhs.

The Sikhs have proud and chivalrous traditions of an intense and compact history, spanning over five centuries. The traits of the Sikhs' native genius, their spirit of faith, service and sacrifice, their cheerful acceptance of God's will (*hukam*) and their readiness to suffer in a righteous cause have formed the bedrock of Sikh History and have enabled them to survive what was perhaps one of the worst religious persecutions in the annals of mankind. Had it not been for the Sikhs, the whole of North India would have been reading the Quran today. Sikh History is replete with martyrdom written in blood. A London padre rightly said, "We spread our religion (Christianity) all over the world by talking about the crucifixion of Christ, your (Sikh) history is full of thousands of Christs." All this forms the noble story of the history of the Sikh peoples' prolonged suffering and resistance and of the eventual triumph it led to.

The history of the Sikhs is a saga of persecution, suffering, chivalry and vicissitudes. It is the story of their trials and tribulations during a prolonged struggle against the oppression, suppression and torture by tyrannical forces. During this long-drawn-out tussle, in those turbulent times; it is initially a tale more of patient suffering and privation than of visible triumph, subsequently resulting in the rise to power and founding of an independent kingdom by the Sikhs. Hereafter it is the fulfillment of aims and aspirations, followed by the collapse of Punjabi nationalism in a clash of arms with the British. Thereafter it recounts the Anglo-Sikh relations; Sikh input and role in the two Great Wars; their contribution in the freedom struggle; fate of the Sikhs during the partition of their homeland in 1947; their position and status in independent India, and finally their present fate and the state to which their leaders have led them. It is replete with the martyrdom and sacrifices of the Sikhs.

The book has been divided in two parts. Part one encapsulates a brief history of the Sikh people and part two gives notes on some salient features requiring more clarification. The endeavour has been to be objective and succinct and the language used is simple, brief and clear, devoid of lengthy details and technicalities. Basically, it is written from a historical and pragmatic point of view and is a statement of facts and figures. If the book proves to be handy and kindles interest in the reader, I will not have labored in vain.

*The book has been written with an open mind. Corrections, criticism and suggestions are welcome.

PROLOGUE

India, a rich land with abundant wealth and natural resources was the insatiable, avaricious booty for pillaging by hordes of conquerors from the North-West. They looted the provinces and left behind devastation and ruin. The hostile races and kingdoms that composed the country were always engaged in internecine strife and on many occasions the rulers invited these invaders to settle personal disputes. Thus, the country was an easy prey to these raiders. The Punjab region which was the main gateway into India was fated to be a perpetual battlefield for hundreds of years. But the people of Punjab, despite suffering the most, refused to learn their lesson from the misery and destruction caused by these invasions.

By the end of the fifteenth century, more than half of the population of Punjab had been converted to Islam, because, since AD 1000 all the invaders had been Muslims. The remaining population remained Hindu and this led to friction, not only between the two religions, but also between the various castes and creeds. Thus, the people continued to remain divided among themselves due to religion and sectarian differences.

The plight of the people and the conditions prevailing in the plains of Punjab, set Guru Nanak (1469 – 1539), thinking. The problem was to unite the people and give them a new standard of loyalties, because they, the people living in Punjab were one people; their God was one and the same, they shared the same ways of life and a common heritage, and their aspirations and aims were also the same. He started a pacifist, reformist movement that ignored parochial differences and emphasized more on broader issues and what they had in common. His movement was a humanitarian one based on the principles of altruism, equality and justice and he emphatically voiced social issues.

The inception of any philosophy, campaign or religion has to be seen in the light of socio-political conditions of the society. Nanak was born a Hindu, but he was also influenced by peace-loving, Muslim pacifist mystics - the Sufi saints. Consequently, his mind-set developed into an **eclectic** state, comprising of the teachings of radical Hindu Bhaktas who had rebelled against the caste-system, ritualism and the intolerance of Brahmanical Hinduism (they all emphasized on the great panacea of the name, oneness of God and equality of man and exhorted people to get rid of priesthood, polytheism and caste system) and the Muslim Sufis who believed in convincing the population by sound logical reasoning and cogent argument rather than by force or threat and vehemently disapproved of iconoclasm of the Muslim conquerors.

Guru Nanak believed in teaching in the language of the people and generally chose Punjabi vernacular (colloquial language - dialects of the fifteenth and sixteenth centuries) instead of Sanskrit for the expression of his ideas, and avoided learned words and metaphysical subtleties. His hallmark was **utter simplicity** so that what he said could be understood by one and all – the rustic and sophisticated alike and never made any claims to kinship with God nor invest his hymns with the garb of sanctity; he was a humble man and content to be a teacher (*guru*).

Guru Nanak took practical steps to break the vicious hold of caste by starting a free community kitchen – *Guru Ka Langar* and persuaded his followers, irrespective of their caste to eat together. He worked ceaselessly for a casteless and egalitarian society and summed up his message in three commandments: *Kirt karo, Naam japo te vand chako* – work, worship, and give in charity. His teachings were cosmic with a message of oneness of humanity that cut across all regions, all caste barriers and all religions. Gradually, Nanak's teachings and his humanitarian and altruistic mission took the shape of an eclectic, non-esoteric and non-denominational faith – the Sikh religion. The entire Sikh theology is based on the philosophy of Baba Nanak. The other Gurus only developed and improved it further as per the prevailing time and conditions.

Sikhism was the combination of the teachings of Sufism, which was rooted in Islamic thought and the Bhakti movement, an organic link to Hindu philosophy. The mystical impulse in Sikhism is surely part of what leads some observers to class it with Hinduism, while the explicit monotheism of the tradition resembles that of Islam. It is by religious origin a purified and protestant development of Hinduism, being nothing more than an attempt to free popular Hinduism of its errors and impurities. It is refined Hinduism purged of its grossness by the more elevated religious precepts of Islam. Sikhism bears to Hinduism much the same relation that Protestantism does to Roman Catholicism. But since the origin and background of the Sikhs was from Hinduism and their customs, practices, culture and life style was deeply embedded in Hinduism; they really could not free themselves from the shackles of their origins and the dominance of Hindu customs and practices, including those which were in direct contravention to the teachings of their gurus. The dividing line is slender and fragile. A close relationship does indeed exist, but there are distinctions as well. Sikh conflict-disagreement with Muslims is on political basis, while that with Hindus is on religious basis. Even Guru Nanak had to combat the furious bigotry of the Muslim and the deep-rooted superstition of the Hindu.

Nanak was followed by nine gurus. The second Guru, Angad (31 March 1504 – 29 March 1552) cultivated and popularized the

Gurumukhi script (earlier called Mahajani or Landa which had evolved out of Sharda or Takri scripts). The third Guru, Amar Das (05 May 1479 – 01 September 1574) introduced social reforms and standardized religious ceremonies; he worked tirelessly and made concerted efforts for the emancipation and empowerment of women. Since he alone could not cater to the needs of thousands of devotees, he increased the number of *manjis* or *parchar kendras* (parishes) to 22 and appointed accomplished agents (*masands*) to organize, worship and collect offerings.

Guru Ram Das, the fourth Guru had a tank dug and started building a town around it. The town initially known after him as *Guru ka Chak*, *Chak Ram Das* or *Ram Das Pura,* is today's Amritsar (the Mecca of the Sikh faith). Guru Arjan Dev (15 April 1563 – 30 May 1606) was the fifth Guru, he completed the tank at Amritsar and built the Golden Temple (Darbar Sahib or Harimandar Sahib) in it. He organized the *masand* system on new lines, the devotees were asked to donate a tithe of their income for humanitarian purposes. His monumental work was the compilation of the Guru Granth (*Adi* Granth) in August 1604 and installing it in the Golden Temple. Since the anthology in the Guru Granth was in Punjabi, it gained enormous popularity among the masses, who did not understand either Sanskrit or Arabic. Guru Arjan was tortured to death (because of his growing popularity and power and refusal to convert to Islam), on 30 May 1606, on the orders of the Mughal emperor, Jahangir.

The martyrdom of Guru Arjan Dev proved to be a turning point in the history of the Sikhs and had far reaching consequences. It altered the course of history. The pacific character of Sikhs changed drastically. This event, more than any other, converted the Sikh community into a warrior commonwealth and made the Sikh religion more popular. Guru Har Gobind (14 June 1595 – 03

March 1644), the next Guru was the first to appeal to arms and raise an army. As the Sikh faith continued to grow, later Mughal emperors viewed the Sikh Gurus as a potential political threat.

In 1675 the ninth Guru was executed for not following the Mughal emperor, Aurungzeb's mandate of converting to Islam, so that it could facilitate him to convert the country to his faith. The slain Guru's son succeeded him; Guru Gobind Singh (1666-1708), the tenth and last Sikh Guru further militarized his followers. In order to fight Mughal tyranny, he raised the Khalsa warrior community (a militant fraternity of saint soldiers) in the spring (*Basakhi*) of AD 1699 and continued to struggle against the Mughals and at times took refuge in the forts and mountains in the North-East of the Punjab. Numerous battles were fought between the Sikhs and local Mughal governors who resorted to disarm them. Tensions subsided as the Mughals became embroiled in internal dynastic conflict.

Aurungzeb brought the Mughal Empire to its maximum territorial extent but its vast armies were diminished and its treasury depleted by the time of his death in 1707. As Guru Gobind Singh travelled to make peace with Aurangzeb's successor, he was assassinated. Before passing away he ordered the Sikhs to abide by the writings in their scriptures, the holy Guru Granth Sahib and that the holy book would succeed him as the Guru.

After the death of Guru Gobind Singh (07 October 1708), the enmity between the Sikhs and the Mughal State became fiercer. The exit of Guru Gobind marked the entry of Banda Singh Bahadur, whom the Guru had asked to continue the tussle against the despotic and ruthless rulers. During the following years the Sikh Khalsa armies under the leadership of General Banda Singh Bahadur carved out a short-lived state in the Punjab. The hereditary aristocracy of the Punjab was abolished and property ownership was granted to anyone who tilled the soil. For six years Banda played merry hell with the Mughal regime. After a siege Banda Bahadur was captured, tortured and executed by the Mughals. The Punjab was recaptured and many Sikh soldiers and civilians were massacred.

The unsuccessful rebellion (1709-1715) by Banda Singh Bahadur against the Mughal rulers of the Punjab was followed by a period of brutal persecution of the Sikhs. Subsequent history is a tale more of suffering than of visible triumph. The Mughal governors were butchers and they persecuted the Sikhs ruthlessly, with savage brutality. Surviving Sikhs again fled to the forts and mountains and for some time, it seemed that the Sikhs had been finished, but then they reappeared and waged a guerilla war against the Mughals. There was duration of continuous but sporadic fighting between the two adversaries; in spite of all the disadvantages the Sikhs were not slow to retaliate whenever the fortune of war favoured them.

By the early 1730s the exhausted Mughals made a short-lived peace with the Sikhs and allowed them to return to settle their lands and a degree of self-rule. In 1739, came the visitation of the Persian invader Nadir Shah of the Saddozai dynasty. He laid the countryside waste and thousands of people were massacred in cold blood. The weakened Mughal Empire's capital city of Delhi was ravaged sacked and plundered of its great wealth. The booty that he carried back comprised a large amount of wealth in addition to the Peacock throne and the most splendid and famous diamond called the "Koh-i-noor," or mountain of light. Shortly afterwards the Marathas subjugated the remnant Mughal Empire as its vassal. Eight years after the conquest of Nadir Shah, came the series of nine invasions (1747 - 1769) by the Afghan Ahmed Shah Abdali/Durrani. The Punjab was overrun by the Afghan armies of

Ahmad Shah Durrani; he defeated the Marathas, who suffered massive casualties at the Third Battle of Panipat (1761). Despite repeated invasions and massacre of Sikh civilians in the latter half of the eighteenth century, the Afghans were never able to wholly subdue the Sikhs. It was during these Afghan invasions that the Sikhs started their upward ascent to power.

Abdali did much to pave the way for a Punjabi State, his repeated incursions compelled the Punjabis to sink their religious quarrels and discrepancies and unite. The invasion of the Abdali, and the occupation of the imperial forces, was favourable to the progress and depredations of the Sikhs, who, often chastised, but never entirely suppressed, now ventured to appear in large bodies, and Sikh plunderers scoured the country in all directions. Since the Sikhs were already fighting the Mughals and Afghans and their resistance was organized, they were able to seize power.

Since the death of Banda Singh Bahadur, the Sikhs were organized in a loose confederation of 12 sovereign communities (called *Misls*), ruled by the Khalsa fraternity of Sikh warriors. After gaining control of eastern Punjab, these small states began fighting against each other whenever not threatened by the Afghans until they were all united by the twenty-year-old war lord, Ranjit Singh. In 1801, he was crowned as the Maharaja of the Sikh empire. He repeatedly defeated the Afghans in major battles, driving their armies out of the Indian sub-continent as far north as the Khyber Pass.

During Maharaja Ranjit Singh's 40 year (1799-1839) long reign, Sikh control expanded over the entire Punjab and Northwest. The complete Punjab was prosperous and internally peaceful. His inclusive, reformed government and military included Sikhs, Hindus, Muslims, European military experts and soldiers of fortune. The army was rigourously trained and modernized specially in the use of artillery. The Sikh Empire only lasted for ten more years after Ranjit Singh's death in 1839. He had maintained peace with the British East India Company that had conquered the Hindu-Maratha confederacy to the South.

The nationalist movement having run its course began to peter out and finally collapsed in the clash of arms with the British. The decade following the demise of the benevolent ruler of Punjab is the sad and squalid narrative of the follies and crimes of the nobles. A crowd of greedy, unscrupulous parasites, who had no thought but of enriching themselves at the expense of the people, were involved in factions, conspiracies, treasons and murders and the princes, ministers and *sardars* were engulfed in this bloody carnage. Betrayal and treachery characterized the men, the Khalsa had so trustingly patronized and raised to the highest civil and military offices. The next three Sikh Maharajas that succeeded Ranjit Singh were all assassinated. The empire was thrown in turmoil as the next Maharaja was a young child. There were disputes, discord and mayhem followed by anarchy which led to the two Anglo-Sikh wars.

The **Anglo-Sikh wars** were the result of British policy of colonial expansion and imperialism. And, looking further in time it was their modus operandi of a planned and visualized system of English capitalizing through loot and exploitation of natural, material and human resources by military hegemony. Ranjit Singh knew all along that the British had an eye on his kingdom. The Sikh army had doubled in size and assumed much of the practical control of the empire. A British observer at the time described the empire as being ruled by a dangerous military democracy. Taking advantage of this internal instability, the British East India Company began amassing troops on the Sikh border. War broke out and after several costly battles, peace was negotiated with the northern territories of Jammu and Kashmir receded to the British, as well as valuable territory in the eastern Punjab. Tensions remained high and a second Anglo-Sikh war broke out only two years later. During the Anglo-Sikh wars the British realized and gave respect to the fighting prowess of the Sikh soldiery. By the end of the wars the British East India Company had usurped the Sikh empire. Lord Dalhousie proclaimed annexation of the Punjab on 29 March 1849.

During the Anglo-Sikh wars, the Sikh army, badly led and deceived, displayed the utmost gallantry in vain. A close scrutiny leaves no doubt that even according to the confessions of responsible adversaries; the Sikhs trounced the British in each and every encounter. In the heat of battle, at the most crucial moment, the treacherous traitors would defect to the British. Most of the battles had been won before the war started. Perhaps, history will never find a better example of such dastardly intrigue and betrayal, where greedy and ungrateful leaders and generals were hell-bent upon destroying their own innocent, faithful and patriotic troops. The Sikh soldiers (simple, loyal and credulous) were defeated not by British skill but by chicanery and the perfidy of their leaders, who deserted them at the crucial juncture, when victory was in their hands. This was followed by persecution of the Sikhs by the British and then came 1857 - the year of the Mutiny, where for obvious reasons, the Sikhs sided with the British. After the Mutiny the Sikhs found themselves no longer regarded with suspicion by the British but treated in a spirit of confidence and good fellowship. They became the most loyal subjects and the sword and shield of the British Empire in India.

Thereafter, it is the Anglo-Sikh relations (sweet and sour). During the following, Company and British colonial rule in India, Sikhs were both feared and respected for their marital ability. Despite only accounting for approximately two percent of India's population, hundreds of thousands of Sikhs served in the army during the British Raj. Sikhs were noted for their loyalty, skill and bravery particularly during the first and second World Wars.

This was followed by Sikh contribution in the freedom struggle of India; fate of the Sikhs during the partition of their homeland in 1947; the raw deal that they got from the government after independence and their position and status in independent India today. After overcoming centuries of adversity, presently there are over twenty-seven million Sikhs worldwide with the majority still living in East/Indian Punjab.

All modes of redressing a wrong having failed,
Raising the sword is just and pious.

- Guru Gobind Singh

THE INVASIONS OF PUNJAB THROUGH THE AGES

Since times immemorial India has been subjected to foreign invasions. Its rich states have been the yearned prize of successive hordes of raiders from the North-West, who have swept over the continent leaving carnage and destruction behind them. When the invaders assaulted the country, because of its geographical location, the first region, they came across was Punjab and it was Punjab that suffered the most at the hands of these intruders. These conquerors came to loot the wealth of Hindustan, since it was a rich country and an easy prey. India was a divided house, the many unfriendly races and nations which made up its population were always engaged in internecine discord. It was difficult for these kingdoms that were always involved in mutual struggles, to withstand the attacks from outside. The rulers of the country had an axe to grind and scores to settle, with each other, in their domestic conflicts. On several occasion, the kings, invited the foreigners in order to sort out their personal differences. When there was a lull in the foreign invasions, they turned against each other.

In AD 712 the first Muslim invasion of India took place, when the Arabian invader Muhammad Bin Kasim (a seventeen-year-old boy) conquered Sind and established Muslim rule there. Sind was set apart from the rest of the country. After AD 1000 all invasions that took place were by Muslim conquerors and gradually, starting from the north, Muslim kingdoms sprang up all over Hindustan. By the end of the fifteenth century **half the population of Punjab had been converted to the faith of the Arabian prophet**.

The foreign invaders at whose hands Punjab had to suffer since the sixth and fifth century BC to the eighteenth-century AD were as follows:

1. According to H.A. Phadke, north-west India was invaded by the Persian Emperors – Cyrus (558-529 BC), Darius (522-486 BC) and Xerxes (486-465 BC). Darius annexed Punjab, west of the Indus and Sind in 518-517 BC.

2. Alexander the Great invaded India in 327-326 BC.

3. Alexander was followed by the Huns (nomad tribes of Central Asia) in the fourth and fifth century AD.

4. Imad-ud-Din Muhammad Bin Kasim conquered Sind in AD 712.

5. Alptgin, a Turkic slave of the Persian King Abdul Malik (d. AD 963) and commander of the Samanid Empire, who later become the semi-independent governor of Ghazni from 962 until his death in 963, attacked India in the ninth century AD.

6. Sabuktigin (942- 997), a slave of Alptgin and later his son-in-law and the Turkish ruler of the kingdom of Ghazni (city located in east-central part of present-day Afghanistan). He was the founder of the Ghaznavid dynasty, ruling from 977 to 997. In Turkic the name means *beloved prince*. He invaded India three times.

7. Sultan Mahmud Ghazni (November 971-30 April 1030), the son of Sabuktigin (a Turkish slave), who ruled Ghazni from 997 to 1030. He invaded Hindustan 17 times, between AD 1000 and 1026.

8. Nearly a hundred and fifty years elapsed before the next invasion of Hindustan. After this respite Mohammad Ghori made several invasions between AD 1175 and 1206.

9. The Mongols attacked India twenty-five times between the thirteenth and fourteenth century AD.

10. Tamerlane (1336-19 February 1405), the Lord of Samarkand (one of the oldest cities of Asia, located in present day Uzbekistan, in the fourteenth century it became the capital of Tamerlane's Mongol empire), who had created an empire, and was successful in every campaign he undertook, invaded India in 1398-99, at the age of 62 and left behind a trail of carnage.

11. Between 1519-26 Zahir-ud-Din Babur (founder of the Mughal dynasty) led five incursions into India.

12. In 1739 came the invasion of the Persian Nadir Shah, during the reign of Muhammad Shah Rangila (1719-48), who was the sixth ruler in the line of eleven lesser/later Mughals. Nadir Shah went through the Punjab, laying waste the country side, as he moved south to Delhi. He plundered Delhi and massacred over 100,000 men, women and children in cold blood. After staying in Delhi for about two months (20 March to 15 May 1740), he left. Nadir Shah is estimated to have carried away booty worth Rs 30 crores, in addition to the Koh-i-noor Diamond and the Peacock Throne. He also took with him thousands of men and women as slaves. The Sikhs, whom every one believed to have been exterminated, reappeared and deprived Nadir Shah of some of his loot and released many of their countrymen from slavery. This act of theirs raised their image in the eyes of the people (including Muslims) and large numbers joined their fraternity.

13. Eight years after the incursion of Nadir Shah, in 1747 came the first of the series of invasions of the Afghan, Ahmed Shah Abdali or Durrani. He invaded India nine times between 1747 and 1767. Each time the Sikh guerillas harassed him and lightened his burden by stripping him of some of the booty that he was carrying home to Afghanistan and also rescuing the captives that he was taking home as slaves. It was during the Afghan invasions (1747-1769) that the Sikhs started their upward ascent to power.

14. Ahmed Shah Abdali's son Taimur Shah invaded India five times between 1774 and 1788-89.

15. Shah Zaman, the son of Taimur Shah and grandson of Ahmed Shah Abdali invaded India four times between 1793 and 1798-99.

Maharaja Ranjit Singh was the first Indian in a thousand years, to stem and reverse the tide of foreign invasions. It was the boast of the northern savages (the Afghans) that grass never grows where their horses have once trodden - Resident Collins. He brought these habitual plunderers of India, the Pathans and Afghans to their knees. When Shah Zaman, during his fourth invasion (January 1799) could not make headway, past the Sikh barricade and proceed to Delhi, he swore to return and teach the Sikhs a lesson in battle and conquer Hindustan. Twelve years later, in 1811, he did come back but not as a conqueror; by a quirk of fate Shah Zaman had been arrested and blinded by his half-brother Mahammad; he then came begging Ranjit Singh for asylum. Soon Zaman's younger brother, Shah Shuja followed in his footsteps and came knocking at the maharaja's door in order to solicit his help in getting back his throne. The large-hearted Ranjit Singh once again showed the generosity and magnanimity for which he was so famous and received Shuja with great courtesy; he gave asylum to the harems of Shuja and the blinded Zaman and granted them a pension.

Zakarya Khan, the governor of Punjab (1726 – 01 July 1745), while witnessing a farce making fun of the Sikhs' boast that they would become rulers of the Punjab, scoffed at them and said, "By God! They live on grass and claim kingship!" (Khushwaqt Rai – Tawarikh-i-Punjab, Page 71). But strange are the ways of providence that can turn kings into beggars, the onetime conqueror of Lahore had come back to the city as a beggar.

The whirligig of time brings its revenges.

- Rommel

PART ONE

IMPORTANT EVENTS IN THE HISTORY OF THE SIKHS

GLIMPSES OF SIKH HISTORY

CHAPTER- 1

RISE TO POWER AND FOUNDING A KINGDOM

BANDA SINGH BAHADUR

Shortly before his death Guru Gobind Singh selected and entrusted Banda Singh Bahadur with the military command of the Sikhs. What surprises historians is the fact that the Guru selected Banda after knowing him for only a month. Banda met the Guru on 03 September 1708 AD and the Guru died on 07 October 1708 AD Guru Gobind Singh was an astute judge of human beings and found in the 38-year-old ascetic Banda (Madho Das/Gurbaksh Singh) all the qualities that he was looking for. Banda was born on 27 October 1670 at Rajauri in the Poonch district of Kashmir. Most of the books say that he was a Rajput and his father Ram Dev, a ploughman. Banda was a gifted man of great learning, "versed in all the ancient wisdom of the Hindus". He had perhaps, acquired certain spiritual powers (*siddhis*) through long hours of yoga and meditation and, with Guru's blessings. Such was the man the Guru chose to lead his people.

Guru Gobind Singh had approached the Emperor Bahadur Shah to seek justice for all the wrong done by the Mughal administration. But having failed, he left the task to Banda Singh Bahadur, of accomplishing by force what appeal to justice had failed to achieve. Banda first fell upon the towns of Kaithal, Samana (it was the residence of Sayyid Jalaluddin the executioner of Guru Tegh Bahadur and Sashal Beg and Bashal Beg the executioners of the two younger sons of Guru Gobind), Shahbad, Ambala (Sadhaura near Ambala was the home town of Usman Khan the man responsible for the execution of Pir Buddhu Shah), and Kapuri and thoroughly plundered them. At Shahdara, the Muslims gave a tough fight, but they were defeated and slaughtered in thousands. This place came to be known as 'Qatalgarhi' (Slaughterhouse) because of this massacre. Then, Sirhind was stormed (1710) and Wazir Khan, the man who had given orders for the murder of the Guru's two younger sons was cut to pieces. The victory at Sirhind was a signal for a general uprising throughout the Punjab. The Sikhs became bold and peasant insurgencies, rebellions and revolts took place in the entire Punjab. The Sikhs captured Amritsar, Kasur, Batala, Kalanaur and Pathankot and looted Lahore to their heart's content. For seven years (1709 – 1715) Banda played merry hell with the decaying Mughal Empire.

Crowds flocked to Banda's camp from all directions to join his standard and seek redressal for wrongs. Banda's role, as assigned by the Guru was limited to that of army commander on a punitive mission, but he took on the spiritual aspect as well. He preached and gave sermons and people came to seek his blessings and ask for boons; he did not disappoint anyone. He was addressed as Guru (something which the Guru had forbidden him to do). **But, having an avowed contempt for worldly goods, he gave away the offerings devotees placed before him.** Heady with success, Banda breathed defiance. Banda was deserted by a large section of the Sikhs who suspected, not without reason that he was trying to invest himself as a Guru. Banda met his Waterloo at Gurdas Nangal in a small fortress called Duni Chand ki Haveli when the Mughal Emperor, Farrukh Siyar (1713-1719) sent his general, Abdul Samad Khan with a large force to crush him. The Mughals besieged the fortress and waited patiently for their victims to starve themselves into submission.

The name of Banda and his Sikhs had become a source of terror, Banda was reputed to be able to deflect a bullet from its course and work such spells that neither spear nor sword could injure his men. Such was the fear of the sorceries of the Sikh chief that the commanders of the Mughal army prayed that God might so ordain things that Banda should seek safety in his flight from the fortress. And so great was the belief in Banda's magical powers and so acute the anxiety to capture him that even dogs and cats that strayed out of his fortress were immediately destroyed (lest Banda may have undergone a feline or canine transformation to make his escape). After eight months of the siege, Banda and his famished, starved and half dead Sikhs surrendered on 12 December 1715 after a promise of good conduct on the Quran, by the Mughals.

According to two historians Irvine and Kamwar, 'The list of arms taken and money seized, does not give a very exalted notion of either the military strength or the wealth of the Sikh leader in the fortress of Gurdas Nangal and it is really astonishing that with so scanty resources the Sikhs so determinedly resisted the greatest Empire of the day for such a long time.'

Abdus Samad Khan started fulfilling his promise by ordering the immediate execution of over two hundred of the vanquished Sikh foe. Banda along with 740 of his companions was imprisoned and sent to Delhi. Zakarya Khan (son of Abdus Samad Khan), the man who escorted the captives to Delhi, rounded up all Sikhs *en route* until he had seven hundred bullock carts full of severed heads and over seven hundred prisoners. On reaching Delhi in end February 1716, the prisoners were made to wear fools' caps on their heads and Banda was dressed in gold brocade to mock his pretentions to kingship and paraded through the streets; they were mocked and jeered by the crowds. Flanking the prisoners were soldiers bearing two thousand Sikh heads belonging to Sikhs who had fallen in battle. An eyewitness described the scene thus: Those unfortunate Sikhs, who had been reduced to this last extremity, were quite happy and contented with their fate; not the slightest sign of dejection or humility was seen in their faces. In fact, most of them, as they passed along on their camels, seemed happy and cheerful, and joyfully singing the sacred hymns of their Scripture (Guru Granth Sahib). And, if anyone from among the crowd called out to them that their own excesses had reduced them to that condition, they quickly retorted saying that it had been so willed by the Almighty and that their capture and misfortune was in accordance with His will. And if anyone said: 'Now you will be killed,' they shouted: "Kill us. When were we afraid of death?" (Mirza Muhammad Harisi in *Ibrat Nama*).

The executions of the Sikhs lasted for a week and were watched by a multitude of crowds including two Englishmen, John Surman and Edward Stephenson. In a report dated 10 March 1716 they have given a detailed description of the scenes and also the equanimity with which the captured Sikhs accepted their fate: '.......... It is not a little remarkable with what patience they undergo their fate, and to the last it has not been found that one apostatized from his new formed religion.' (*Early Records of British India*, p.180 – J.T. Wheeler). Even the author of *Siyar-ul-Mutakherin* admitted reluctantly that "these people not only behaved firmly during the execution, but they would dispute and wrangle with each other for priority in execution" (p.79).

Many tales of whole-hearted devotion of the Sikh prisoners to their Guru and leader and steadfastness to their faith are told and many who were not eyewitness to them were inclined to dismiss them as incredible, says Khafi Khan. Among the prisoners was a tender aged, newly married boy, who had been arrested from a village on the way. His widowed mother followed the prisoners all the way to Delhi. As tutored, she pleaded with the emperor and told him that her son was not a Sikh, but a prisoner in the hands of the Sikhs. On procuring the order of release, she ran and gave it to the officer in charge of the executions. The boy was summoned and told that since he was not a Sikh, he was free. The lad said that his mother was a liar. No amount of persuasion by the State officers and wailing, lamenting or beseeching by the mother could move him. He ran back to the place of execution, where he was beheaded (Tarikh-i-Muhammad-Shahi).

After the execution of his comrades, Banda's execution was the most excruciating and gruesome of them all. He was very cruelly and brutally butchered to death on 09 June 1716. Banda was seated on the ground and offered the usual choice between Islam and death, but the devoted follower of Guru Gobind Singh preferred death over abjuring his faith. Thence, Banda Singh's four-year-old son, Ajay Singh was placed in his arms and he was ordered to take the infant's life. He refused. Therefore, the executioner cut the child to pieces, gouged out his quivering heart and thrust it into the father's mouth, who stood unmoved; absolutely still like a statue, completely resigned to God's will.

Thereafter, came Banda Singh Bahadur's turn. His right eye was removed by the point of a butcher's knife followed by the left. Next, his left foot was chopped off, and then his hands were severed from his body. Banda's flesh was torn from his body with red hot pincers, and finally he was decapitated and hacked to pieces.

Banda's fight was against the Muslim ruling class, but his last words were not of hatred against the Muslims. He said: 'Whenever men like you become so corrupt and wicked as to relinquish the path of equity and abandon themselves to all kinds of excesses, then providence sends a scourge like me to chastise them; when the quantum punishment is complete, then He raises men like you to punish men like me.'

Two and a half years following the execution of Banda Singh Bahadur, Emperor Farrukh Siyar (the third in the line of the eleven lesser or later Mughals), who had come to power after getting his uncle Jahandar Shah, the king, suffocated to death and the man who had ordered Banda's execution, met an equally tragic death at the hands of his own people, when he was pulled down from his throne; bare headed and bare footed he was dragged, beaten, abused and made a captive. He was starved, blinded, poisoned and ultimately suffocated to death in February 1719.

It was Banda Singh, who laid the foundation of the Sikh empire and sovereignty in Punjab, in 1710. It was through Banda Singh that the path to conquest was discovered by the Khalsa. He was the first man to deal a severe blow to the intolerant rule of the Mughals in Punjab. He was a great political leveler and an admirable social uplifter. Banda was a remarkable man; it is sad that he was murdered at the age of 45, for had he lived longer he would have done wonders, yet he achieved so much with so little and in such a short time. Banda could not give the Sikhs a permanent kingdom, but he achieved much more - he changed the course of history of Punjab; woke the people from their deep slumber and taught the Sikhs some very vital lessons. His biggest gift was **unity** and how powerful common people can be in big numbers when they come together and stand united in solidarity against a mighty and ruthless enemy. He showed them the difference between those in power and those who were out of it. He taught them that no people could become a great nation without sacrifice and shedding blood and the importance of self-reliance, resilience, courage and industry. These lessons, taught practically could not be ignored by a militant community battling for its survival. Their grim struggle was ultimately rewarded and, in less than half a century, the Sikhs became the undisputed masters of Punjab.

What the Sikhs hold against Banda Bahadur is his haughtiness (a little pride is but natural in human nature) and his surrender to the enemy, when he should have died fighting. Muslim writers describe Banda as a great tyrant. But to the Hindus and Sikhs he was a great soldier, a brave general and an able administrator. He was champion of their liberty and protector of their faith. He saved the Hindus from oppression by replying to the tyranny of the Mughals in their own language and it was through him that the people of Punjab discovered their latent potential and the path to conquest and freedom.

PERSECUTION OF SIKHS (1716-1765)

After Banda Singh Bahadur the persecution of Sikhs started on a large scale and for the first five years after Banda's execution very little was heard of them. The Sikhs again came under sword and fire for another half a century, first by Mughal kings and later by the Afghan King, Ahmad Shah Abdali. They were hunted like animals by the Mughals and a price was laid on their heads. Since the Khalsa were easily identifiable by their long hair and flowing beards, the only choice left to them was either to give up the external emblems of their faith or keep out of the way of Mughal soldiers. Many succumbed to the terror which was let loose and became clean-shaven (*sahajdhari*) and many who were determined to remain Khalsa fled to inaccessible areas of the hills, jungles and deserts leaving their lands and women folk in the care of relatives. They were outlaws and men at large, living off the land and existing on plunder. Under the prevailing conditions, the Sikhs became reckless and an attitude of couldn't careless pervaded over these desperados. They developed a behavior of indifference to worldly possessions and an instinct for gambling with their lives against odds. The repression of the Sikhs proved to be a blessing in disguise. The most important result of this policy of repression was to uproot as many peasants from the land and convert them into professional soldiers. Thus, the Sikhs were provided with a standing army with an intimate knowledge of the area of operation and a continuing connection with the peasantry.

The literal and practical meaning of the words annihilate, eliminate, eradicate, extirpate, exterminate, and wipe out as understood from the dictionary were vividly applicable to the Sikhs because there were large scale genocides, holocausts, massacres and pogroms of the Sikhs. Oppression, suppression, repression and exploitation are the precise words as to what was happening to them during these decades of persecution. There were times in between when they had the upper hand. Far from terrorizing them this hardened their stand all the more. And as is usual in times of adversity strong bonds of brotherhood and bonhomie grew amongst the Sikh exiles. There was a lot of fraternity, camaraderie and esprit de corps.

CHHOTA GHALLUGHARA (Lesser Holocaust or Carnage, 01-02 May 1746)

Jaspat Rai, the Mughal *faujdar* (administrator or official who had troops under him for maintaining law and order) of Eminabad, 55 km north of Lahore, was killed in an encounter with a roving band of Sikhs. Jaspat Rai's brother, Lakhpat Rai, who was a *diwan* (revenue minister) at Lahore, vowed revenge and promised to scourge the entire Sikh p*anth* (community) out of existence. As an immediate first step, he **had the Sikh inhabitants of Lahore rounded up and killed in a general massacre**. On 10 March 1746, the governor Yahya Khan and Lakhpat set out at the head of a large force, mostly cavalry supported by cannon, in search of Sikhs concentrated in the swampy forest of Kahnuvan, 15 km south of the present town of Gurdaspur. The forest was surrounded. The Sikhs held out for some time, striking back whenever they could. But heavily outnumbered and underequipped, they decided to make a dash for the hills in the northeast. On crossing the river Ravi, they found their way blocked by hostile Rajput hill men. Caught in this situation, they suffered heavy casualties. Some fought their way through and escaped to the mountains. Making a last desperate surge, the remaining survivors broke through the encirclement and succeeded in re-crossing the river Ravi, though many were carried away by the torrent. With Lakhpat Rai still close at their heels, they crossed the Beas and the Sutlej to find refuge in their old sanctuary, the Lakhi jungle, deep into the Malwa region. **An estimated 7,000 Sikhs were killed and 3,000 captured** in this action fought on 01 and 02 May 1746. Lakhpat Rai marched back in triumph to Lahore where **he had the captives beheaded in batches** in the *Nakhas* (site of horse market) outside the Delhi gate. Lakhpat Rai ordered Sikh places of worship to be destroyed and their holy books burnt. The total number of Sikhs martyred was more than 10,000. It was a bloodbath and brutal killing of helpless Sikhs.

The number of Sikhs massacred during the *Chhota Ghallughara* was much more than the *Vadha Ghallughara*, but it is known as *Chhota* or small because historians count the deaths in a single day i.e., ten thousand (01 and 02 May 1746) as compared to thirty thousand (05 February 1762). The *Chhota Ghallughara* lasted for a number of months whereas the *Vadha Ghallughara* lasted for a single day. The death toll before and after the fateful, horrid day of 01-02 May 1746 are not taken into account.

Far from being wiped out, within six months of the holocaust the Sikhs were back again, with their *jathas* (bands) knocking at the doors of Amritsar from various directions. They celebrated the Baisakhi of 1747, at Amritsar and, also built a mud fortress – Ram Rauni (named in honour of the founder of the city, Guru Ram Das) just outside Amritsar. When Mir Manu became the governor of Lahore in March 1748, he appointed Kaura Mal (a *Nanakpanthi, Sahajdhari* Sikh) as his deputy and *diwan* (revenue minister). Kaura Mal paid balance of the fine (Rs 10 lakh) levied on Lakhpat Rai and obtained permission of Mir Manu to take custody of him. As a reprisal for his cruelty on the Sikhs, Diwan Kaura Mal handed over Diwan Lakhpat Rai to the Dal Khalsa (Khalsa army). He was thrown into a dungeon where he died a miserable death after six months of indignity and torture (1748). It may be noted that Diwan Kaura Mal is an ancestor of the famous Sikh poet, scholar, and exegete Bhai Vir Singh (1872-1957). Bhai Vir Singh is accredited to be the creator of modern Punjabi literature and a prominent figure of Singh Sabha Movement.

VADHA GHALLUGHARA **(The Great Holocaust or Carnage - 05 February 1762)**

Ahmad Shah Abdali/Durrani was getting fed up with the harassment and activities of the Sikhs who were getting bolder day by day. On his return home after his historic victory over the Marathas in 1761 (his fifth invasion), the Sikhs had liberated over two thousand Hindu women Abdali was taking home to stock Afghan harems and harassed him all the way from river Sutlej right up to the river Indus. Returning to the Central Punjab, they ravaged the country all around, annihilated the Afghan force in Char Mahal, drove away the *faujdar* of Jalandhar, plundered Sirhind and Malerkotla, defeated a 12,000 strong force sent by Ahmad Shah from Afghanistan to punish the Sikhs and also another force led personally by the Afghan governor of Lahore. They even went and captured Lahore. All this happened within a short span from June – September 1761.

At a general assembly of the Sarbat Khalsa (commonwealth of Sikhs) convened on the occasion of Diwali, 27 October 1761, it was resolved to punish the agents, informers and collaborators of the Afghans, beginning with Aqil Das of Jandiala, head of the heretical Niranjania sect and an inveterate enemy of the Sikhs. Aqil Das dispatched messengers post haste to Ahmad Shah Durrani, who had in fact already entered India on his sixth invasion, at the head of a large army. But before he could reach Jandiala, 18 km east of Amritsar, the Sikhs had lifted the siege and retired beyond the Sutlej with the object of sending their families to the safety of the wastelands of Malwa before confronting the invader.

Ahmad Shah on the other hand, determined to teach the Sikhs a lesson, sent messages to Zain Khan, *faujdar* of Sirhind, and Bikhan Khan, chief of Malerkotla, directing them to immediately check the advance of the Sikhs. He himself set out at once with a light cavalry force and covering a distance of 200 km including two river-crossings in less than forty-eight hours, caught up with the Sikhs who were camping at Kup-Rahira, 12 km north of Malerkotla, at dawn on the 5th of February 1762. The Dal Khalsa comprising all the eleven *misls* (Sikh confederacies) and representatives of Sikh chiefs of Malwa was taken by surprise. The attacks of Zain Khan and Bhikhan Khan were repulsed, but the main body of Ahmad Shah, much larger and better equipped soon overtook them.

Having to protect the slow-moving *vahir* (baggage train comprising of women, children, old people and other non-combatants); the Sikhs could not resort to their usual hit-and-run tactics. On the advice of Sardar Jassa Singh Ahluwalia, the commander of the Dal Khalsa, they formed a cordon around the *vahir* and thus fighting while marching, they headed towards Barnala, 40 km to the southwest, with the agents of the Malwa chiefs acting as guides. At Barnala they expected Ala Singh of

Patiala (head of the twelfth Sikh *misl*) to come to their rescue. On several occasions, the Shah's troops broke the cordon and butchered the helpless non-combatants, but every time the Sikh warriors re-formed and pushed back the attackers. The Afghans took a heavy toll of Sikh lives and by early afternoon they reached a big pond, the first water body they had come across during the day. The fighting stopped automatically as the two forces (man and beast) fell pell-mell, upon the water to quench their thirst and relax their tired limbs. The battle was not resumed.

The Sikhs marched off towards Barnala and Ahmad Shah thought it prudent not to pursue them in the little-known semi-desert with an army that had had no rest during the past two days and had suffered considerable loss of life in the day-long battle. The original version of the Adi Granth recompiled by Guru Gobind Singh was lost in this engagement. The troubles of the Sikhs were not yet over. Those who eluded the Afghans had to run the gauntlet of the Brar tribes, who turned against them. Ala Singh failed to come to the help of his co-religionists. Nevertheless, he was taken prisoner by the Afghans, and Barnala, which was in his territory, was burned down. His life was spared by his protesting his neutrality and paying a tribute of five lakh of rupees and another one and a quarter lakh to appear before the Shah with his beard and hair unshorn. The Rohilla chief Najibuddaulah interceded on his behalf.

Abdali returned to Lahore with fifty cart loads of heads and hundreds of Sikhs in chains. According to Foster, "Pyramids were erected and covered with the heads of slaughtered Sikhs: and it is mentioned that Ahmad Shah caused the walls of those mosques, which the Sikhs had polluted, to be washed with their blood so that they could be decontaminated, and the ignominy offered to the religion of Muhammad be expiated." From Lahore Abdali went to

Amritsar and again blew up the Harimandar Sahib with gun powder and filled the pool with carcasses of cows.

A conservative estimate of the loss of Sikh lives is between twenty-five and thirty thousand (mostly non-combatants). This could have been a crippling blow to the Sikhs, but such was the state of their morale that in a gathering in the evening that same day a Nihang Sikh stood up and proclaimed aloud, "…. the fake has been shed. The true Khalsa remains intact." The Sikhs rose again within three months to attack Zain Khan of Sirhind, who bought peace by paying Rs 50,000 in May, and they were ravaging the neighbourhood of Lahore during July-August 1762. Ahmad Shah was still in the Punjab and he watched helplessly the devastation of the Jalandhar Doab at their hands. From the foresaid it is apparent that the casualties were mostly non-combatants. The holocaust of 05 February 1762 is known to the Sikhs as the *Vada Gallughara* (the Great Massacre).

THE *MISL* PERIOD (1765 – 1799)

According to the Encyclopedia of Sikhism, *Misl* is a term which originated in the eighteenth-century history of the Sikhs to describe a unit or brigade of Sikh warriors and the territory acquired by it in the course of its campaign of conquest following the weakening of the Mughal authority in the country. There are many conjectures by historians about the etymology of the word *misl* generally based on the Arabic/Persian word *misl*. The various meanings are: similitude, alike or equal; a file or collection of papers bearing on a particular topic; a tribe or race; a voluntary association of the Sikhs; territory conquered by a brave Sikh *Sardar* with the help of his comrades; *derah* or encampment; a *thana* or military/police post; a friendly nation; a brotherhood; a confederacy of clans under their respective chiefs leagued together; a *maslahat* or a front–garrison, a border fortification, warlike (people), armed (men), guards, guardians and so on. *Misl* in the meaning of a file or record (maintained according to some, at *Akal Takht*, under the commander of the entire Sikh army, the ***Dal Khalsa***) pertaining to a Sardar's fighting force and territorial acquisitions has been mentioned by Sita Ram Kohli and J. D. Cunningham has taken note of this connotation of the word too.

In order to understand the genesis and evolution of the *misl* system in a historical perspective, we must go back to the beginning of the eighteenth century. With the execution of Banda Bahadur, the Sikhs were hunted out of their homes. They scattered in small *jathas (*bands/groups) to find refuge in distant hills, forests and deserts, but they were far from vanquished. Armed with whatever weapons they could lay their hands upon and living off the land, these highly mobile guerilla *jathas* remained active during the worst of times. The *jathas* or fighting bands under their *jathedars* (*sardars*/leaders/chiefs of *jathas*) functioned independently, but it was not unusual for them to combine with one another when the need arose, or the situation so demanded or if it was profitable. It was also customary for *jathas* to congregate at Amritsar to celebrate *Baisakhi* and *Diwali.* The biannual general assembly meeting (at Basakhi and Diwali) of the Sikh ***panth*** (community of Sikh people) at the Golden Temple in Amritsar is called ***Sarbat Khalsa*** (commonwealth of Sikhs). Any decision taken or resolution passed by the Sarbat Khalsa was known as ***gurmata*** (this was binding on all Sikhs) and the combined force (synergy) of all the *Jathas*/groups/bands/*misls* under a unified command was called the ***Dal Khalsa*** (Sikh army). Thus, the *misls* were collectively known as *Dal Khalsa.*

In consideration of administrative convenience, Nawab Kapur Singh (elected commander of the *Dal Khalsa*) divided the entire body of troops into two camps, called *Buddha Dal* (army of elders or veterans) and *Taruna Dal* (army of the young), respectively. *Taruna Dal* was further divided into five *jathas*, each with its own flag and drum. Under pressure of renewed persecution, the Khalsa was again forced to split into smaller groups. Up to 1,745 roving bands or *jathas* of a dozen or more horsemen under a *jathedar* were operating independently. Following the death of Zakariya Khan (governor of Punjab) on 01 July 1745, the Sikhs gathered at Amritsar for *Diwali* and reorganized themselves into 25 *jathas*, each with 100 horses. The old division into the *Buddha* and *Taruna Dals* was maintained, but the new *deras* (camp or habitation) generally belonged to the latter. The *dera*s spread quickly. By March 1748 there were 65 groups operating in different parts of the Punjab. They carried out their operations generally independent of one another, though they still acknowledged the pre-eminent position of Nawab Kapur Singh. On *Baisakhi*, 29 March 1748, the *Sarbat Khalsa* decided to offer organized resistance to Mughal oppression under the *Dal Khalsa* commanded by Sardar Jassa Singh Ahluwalia. A *gurmata* (resolution) was passed and the 65 bands were reduced and grouped into 11 *misls* (Sikh confederacies) each under its *sardar* or chief.

The eleven *misls* were: Ahluwalia, Singhpuria (aka Faizulapuria), Karorsinghia, Nishananwali, Shahid, Dallewalia, Shukerchakia, Bhangi, Kanhaiya, Nakkai and Ramgarhia. The first six *misls* were under *Buddha Dal* and the latter five under *Taruna Dal*. Jassa Singh Ahluwalia (the chief of Ahluwalia *misl*) was chosen to be in joint command of the entire *Dal Khalsa*, while Nawab Kapur Singh the chieftain of the Singhpuria *misl* continued to be acknowledged as the supreme commander. The combined *Misls* formed the *Dal Khalsa* or Sikh army. The twelfth *misl* was **Phulkian** under Baba Ala Singh of Patiala, but it was not a part of the *Dal Khalsa* command. At least 7 of the 12 Sikh *Misls* were led by Jat-Sikhs.

As mentioned above, the Arabic word *misl* means "like." The Sikh *misls* were "alike" in the sense that they were considered equals. Their fighting strength was, however, far from equal. Some had only a few hundred men; others, like the Bhangis, could put more than ten thousand soldiers in the field. Colonel Polier, a Swiss, described the *misls* as "that formidable aristocratic republic" of Sikh soldiers who are "indefatigable; mounted on the best horses that India can afford……Fifty of them are enough to keep at bay a whole battalion of the King's forces." (Asiatic Annual Register, 1800, pp. 34-35). The *misls* were subject to the control of the *Sarbatt Khalsa* (the biannual assembly of the *panth* at Amritsar). The *Sarbatt Khalsa* was a central forum of the *panth*. It had to elect a leader of the *Dal Khalsa*, and to lay down its political goal and plans of its military strategy, besides adjudicating disputes about property and succession. The Akal Takht was the symbol of the unity of the *Dal Khalsa* which was in a way the Sikh state in making.

The *Dal Khalsa*, mainly a cavalry force was a kind of a loose confederacy, without any regular constitution. The strength of the *misls* varied from time to time. It is estimated that the total strength that the Dal Khalsa could muster was about seventy thousand (70,000) horse and foot. Every *misl* was sovereign. The chief maintained his independent character and exercised full authority within his domain. The *khalsa* (sovereign) or crown lands remained under the direct control of the *misl* chief. Their armies were unencumbered by heavy ordnance and possessed amazing speed and maneuvering ability. With their scanty accoutrement, they could cover from 100 to 200 km daily for days and could encamp and decamp in a few minutes. The *misl* soldier was adept in predatory warfare which could earn him a share in booty, for he got no salary. All Khalsa Sikhs had the option to join or quit any of the *misls* they liked. The Dal Khalsa established its authority over most of the Punjab region in a short time. By the 1770s, Sikh hegemony extended from the Indus in the west to the Yamuna in the east, from Multan in the south to Jammu in the north. But the Sikhs, like the Marathas, were a loose, disunited and quarrelsome conglomerate of 12 kin-groups.

By displaying a rare spirit of magnanimity towards the erstwhile persecutors of their faith, by supporting the cause of the poor, the helpless and the innocent and by preserving social and economic equality in their ranks the Sikh *misls* made Sikh religion popular with the young and daring men in the villages. The main source of income of the *misl* in the initial stages was plunder, augmented later by *rakhi* imposts. *Rakhi* (protection) was, like the *chauth* of the Marathas, a levy of a portion, usually one-fifth of the revenue assessment of a territory, as a fee for the guarantee of peace and protection. It was during this period that the word ***Sardar*** for the Khalsa Sikhs came into vogue. Initially only the heads/leaders of the *jathas* (roving bands) which later combined to form *misls* were called *sardars*. Duties on traders and merchants also brought some revenue. The Sikh *misls* were republican in character and elected their chiefs, but gradually they acquired a hereditary footing.

The *misldari* system had worked well under leaders like Nawab Kapur Singh and Jassa Singh Ahluwalia. It ideally suited the times and conditions that prevailed. It combined freedom of action with the discipline of a unified command. Most importantly it channeled the energies of the wild and fiercely independent Khalsa soldier in the service of a cause that he dearly espoused – the banishment of aliens from the soil of the Punjab and the accomplishment of the prophecy of their Guru of the establishment of a Khalsa state.

Adversity, unity of purpose and a common enemy had kept the Sikh *misls* united. With the crumbling of the Mughal Empire and when the Afghan threat receded, the Sikh *sardars* started fighting among themselves, and became soldiers of fortune. Now that there was no danger from abroad and plenty of land to appropriate, the *misl* organization began to lack cohesion. Sikh *misls* became a divided house; they had no love lost for each other; they operated independently. It led to the break-up of the *misls*.

During this period of upheaval when the Sikhs were at each other's throat, there was a silver lining in the dark cloud that had cast its shadow over the Sikh horizon. This consoling or hopeful prospect was the *Sahid* or *Nihang misl* and a selfless man called Sahib Singh Bedi. The service of the *Sahid* or *Nihang misl* was completely selfless, as the leaders of this misl did not occupy any territory. When the fratricidal wars started among the Sikh *misls*; the *Nihangs* remained aloof and neutral, refusing to raise their weapons against fellow Sikhs. But whenever and wherever any *misl* faced a non-Sikh enemy, the brave men of this *misl* fought with unmatched valour, and helped keep the Sikh flag (*Nishan Sahib*) flying high. After the battle they would always retire to their camps and immerse themselves in their religious duties. Sahib Singh Bedi (1756 – 1834) was tenth in direct descent from Guru Nanak. By virtue of his descent from the holy Guru and his age, he enjoyed the status of father of the Sikhs. Sahib Singh Bedi was revered by the Sikh masses for his piety and prowess. He was always wont to appear as a saviour when the Sikhs were in a crisis and threatened with disruption. The venerable Sahib Singh Bedi united the Sikhs when there were differences between them and stopped them from being misled by the enemy when he was trying to sow seeds of discord among them. Such was the prestige of the man that the ***Sardars*** obeyed without demur; they readily and implicitly agreed to abide by his decision.

The chief cause for discord between the *misls* was the relaxation of external pressure and the love of loot. The *misls*, during this time were involved in internecine scuffle, and it was difficult for them to think of common interests and gains and look into the future. **It proved to be the degradation of the *misls* from contingents of freedom fighters to looters and, also the undoing of the Sikhs and their unique institution, the *Dal Khalsa*.** It was evident now that the *misls* had seen their day and, if Punjab was to remain free, it had to be united under one man. The name of this man was Ranjit Singh. He brushed aside all opposition; overpowered and united the warring factions of the Punjab and created a mighty and well-knit Sikh empire.

MAHARAJA RANJIT SINGH (13 November 1780 – 27 June 1839)

Maharaja Ranjit Singh belonged to the Shukerchakia *misl*. He liquidated the warring *misls* and united them into the *Khalsa* brotherhood. After achieving supremacy over the other *misls* he built up a kingdom in Punjab, which subsequently spread to Kashmir and the Frontier Province. Thus, he became the founder and maharaja (1801-1839) of the Sikh kingdom of Punjab. He developed a formidable fighting force in which brave men demonstrated a resolute spirit and unmatched selflessness. In 1799 he seized Lahore; in 1802 he captured Amritsar, it was Multan in 1818, and then Kashmir in 1819. By 1820 he had consolidated his rule over the whole of Punjab between the Sutlej and Indus rivers. In 1823 he decimated the Afghan and Pathan forces and the whole of the North–West Frontier Province right up to the Khyber Pass passed under Sikh control. For the first time in two thousand years of the history of Hindustan, he turned the tide of invasion and brought the traditional conquerors of India, the Afghans and Pathans to their knees. Maharaja Ranjit Singh is included in the list of "Undefeated Military Commanders", who did not lose any significant engagement against the enemy.

Capital punishment was unknown in Ranjit Singh's kingdom. Throughout his life he never passed a single sentence of death. He abolished the death sentence for every crime, however heinous it might be. Crime was generally atoned with fines. Fine (determined not according to the gravity of the crime but by the capacity of the criminal to pay) was the general mode of punishment and in criminal cases the punishment was quick and summary. "Never was so large an empire founded by one man with so little criminality," says Princep. "Except in actual warfare," writes Osborne, who visited him, "he has never been known to take life, though his own has been attempted more than once, and his reign will be found freer from any striking acts of cruelty and oppression than those of many more civilized monarchies." He built up a kingdom and a powerful army and yet he disliked bloodshed. Despite his many conquests, he did not allow any wanton destruction of life or property.

Ranjit Singh was an individual with modern vision and leadership. He had failings and vices like the other contemporary kings of his time; the love of wine, women and horses remained with Ranjit Singh throughout his life; nevertheless, he was a remarkable man. Though illiterate, he was extremely brave and very inquisitive. Ranjit Singh was a monarch of a secular state. His government was known as Sarkar-e-Khalsa because it belonged to the entire Khalsa. His kingdom was ruled through his subjects Hindu, Muslim, Sikh and Christian alike. They were chosen men of talent and ability, who controlled Ranjit's civil administration and the army. Merit and efficiency were the main criterion of his selection and not caste, creed or religion. These men were loyal to him as long as he lived. He was remarkably humane, liberal and benevolent. He was simple in his habits, courteous in speech and utterly humble in his dealings. He respected religious men. Even at the height of his power, he did not lose the common touch. Ranjit Singh's love of the arts was equally well marked. He employed artists in his court and during his campaigns gave orders to his generals to take every care to spare libraries and other places of art. This was the golden era of Sikh history, a period of glory and splendour; the Sikh Kingdom was at the height of its sovereignty. It was the time when Sikh arms had attained their greatest power, the Sikh commonwealth its widest expansion and the Sikh religion had its prominence.

No doubt, Maharaja Ranjit Singh was a remarkable monarch. He was an extraordinary man and an enlightened king with a charismatic personality. He was a glittering, exotic sovereign of his time and had a large heart of gold. Endowed with visionary statesmanship and warriors' valour, he evoked intense loyalty among his subjects and his army consisting of Sikhs, Rajputs, Hindus and Muslim. He never admitted the possibility of failure, and hence held the "awe factor". His subjects loved him and were loyal to him till the last breath of his life.

But alas! He had not trained his progeny to become rulers. He could not distinguish some of his true friends and well-wishers from the flatters, shrewd and scheming men who surrounded him. They were all pliable sycophants, hypocrites and ungrateful upstarts whom he had brought from outside. Ultimately, after his death they all betrayed his trust. The three quislings Tej Singh, Lal Singh and Gulab Singh proved to be the worst and the most cunning and shrewd of them all. They hunted with the hound and ran with the hare. His people were simple, gullible, mostly illiterate, and quick tempered. They were crude and rough by tongue, but clear at heart. They were straight forward and blunt Punjabis, who did not mince words and believed in calling a spade a spade. The Maharaja kept them at bay in far off places and allowed the Purbias and Dogras to associate with him and run the day-to-day affairs of the state. Ultimately after his demise, this inability to recognize fair weather friends and differentiate them from the true ones proved to be the undoing of the mighty empire which he had painstakingly built with so much toil and sweat.

CHAPTER- 2

DOWNFALL OF THE SIKHS AND BRITISH RULE

ANGLO-SIKH WARS

The wars were the result of British policy of colonial expansion and imperialism and looking further in time it was the British policy of planned and visualized British colonial hegemony. Ranjit Singh knew that the British had an eye on his kingdom. The Maharaja was once shown a map of India, where the British possessions were marked in red colour. On scanning the map with his single eye, he saw the whole of Hindustan except Punjab painted red. He turned to his courtiers and remarked: "One day it will all be red." It took only **ten years** for the maharajah's prophecy to be fulfilled. Though Ranjit Singh employed a lot of European officers, his attitude towards them and the English was consistently distrustful. He is known to have remarked, "All of these *feringhees* (Europeans) are *haramzadas* – bastards." As long as he lived, he knew how to deal with the British and they knew how to tackle him. If he was cautious of the British, they too knew his strength and the loyalty of his subjects. But as soon as he died, everything turned topsy-turvy, his kingdom was in turmoil. There were factions, conspiracies, treasons and murders and the princes, ministers and Sardars were engulfed in this bloody carnage. The British set spies and traitors to work to create conditions favourable for a successful occupation of the country. A number of his top officers fell prey to temptation and sided with the British. They had turned double-dealers. They were Tej Singh (1799-1862) a Gaur Brahmin turned Sikh from Meerut district, and Lal Singh (died 1866) a Brahmin of Sanghoi in Jehlum district of West

Punjab (now Pakistan), the European officers, the Hindustani sepoys (employed in the Durbar's forces and known to Punjabis as *purabiah-easterner*-or by the name *Mata Din*), the Dogra brothers, and the Sandhawalia Sardars.

The simple, naïve and gullible Sikhs were no match to the astute and shrewd British. The English had taken the Cis-Sutlej Sikh states under their protection and built a cantonment at Ludhiana. They moved guns, stores, munitions and troops from Ambala, Meerut and some other stations to the Sikh frontier and openly provoked the Sikhs. During the **First Anglo-Sikh War** five battles were fought – Mudki (18 December 1845), Ferozshahr (21 December 1845), Baddowal (21 January 1846), Aliwal (28 January 1845) and Sobraon (10 February 1846). The Punjabis fought with their usual spirit of courage, chivalry and patriotism and came very close to victory at some decisive moments. But the last-minute desertions and treacheries by their crafty commanders Tej Singh and Lal Singh saved the British many a desperate situation. Both the Sikh commanders Lal Singh and Tej Singh, Raja Gulab Singh Dogra, many of the chieftains, both Sikh and Dogra and the Europeans were in secret treasonable communication with the English and in all probability Rani Jind Kaur (the widow of Maharaja Ranjit Singh) was aware of it. They were willing to sell out Punjab provided their lives and *jagirs* (estate – large land holding bestowed by the king for services rendered) were secured and they fulfilled their treacherous promises to the English. The worst part was played by the three quislings Tej Singh, Lal Singh and Gulab Singh Dogra. The Sikh soldiers were lions being led by sheep and were defeated not by British skill but by the treachery of their leaders.

After the First Anglo-Sikh War the traitors were rewarded by the English for their infidelity and ignoble and dastardly services that they had rendered them and the *sardars* who had dared so much in the field of battle, showed surprising timidity in the political arena; they were brilliant leaders in war, but incapable of handling the reigns of civil government. They requested the wily traitor Raja Gulab Singh to negotiate for them. This suited the British because he was their stooge and would do their bidding. The British took over the Punjab and a caretaker government was installed, vide the treaty of Lahore on 09 and 11 March 1846 and ultimately a fresh Treaty of Bharowal on 16 December 1846. The British sold Jammu and Kashmir (J & K) to Gulab Singh for 75 lakh rupees and recognized him as Maharaja of J & K.

Lord Hardinge (1844-48), the *tundalat* (one-armed Lord) had already made up his mind about the future of the Sikh kingdom. He knew that there were still far too many Khalsa soldiers scattered about in the country to permit annexation; so, he contended himself with terms which would facilitate a take-over at a more appropriate time. The Sikh Kingdom was weakened by depriving it of valuable territory and reducing its army. The **Second Anglo Sikh War** was in fact a national revolt against the intentional provocations and highhandedness of the British.

During the Second Anglo Sikh War, two battles were fought at Challianwala and Gujrat. After the second battle at Gujrat (21 February 1849), the British annexed Punjab and thereafter the persecution of the Sikhs at the hands of the British commenced. What happened to the Sikhs was their own doing (mainly that of their leaders). They brought ruin upon themselves. They could have easily defeated the *feringhee*, but their leaders were busy settling scores with each other and their infidelity due to cupidity for mammon had turned several of them into treacherous turncoats and deceivers. The Sikhs lacked patriotic, honest, courageous, competent, and clear-headed leadership. There was not one wise man among them. A tree grows from the bottom but dries from the top.

BRITISH SHREWDNESS AND SUPPRESSION OF SIKHS

It seems clear that India became a prey to foreign conquest because of the inadequacy of her own people and because the British represented a higher and advancing social order. For the British, ends justified the means and they used all weapons in their arsenal to achieve this. It was an invariable custom with the English first to gain a footing by the excitement of avarice, by the promise of assistance or other flattering terms, and then by gradual steps to assume the government of the country. The British were unscrupulous schemers, skilled in the craft of giving graft and corrupting the locals. They bribed and depraved the ministers and other officials. They were past masters in the art of intrigue, subversion, deceit and the use of spies and fifth columnists. Their spy system was perfect and functioned continuously; in moments of crisis and in the heat of war there would be defections in their favour which made a great difference. They won most of their battles before the actual fighting took place.

It goes to the credit of the British (a nation of petty shop keepers) for having overrun a vast subcontinent with a handful of traders from the British East India Company, who had come to trade in India. They used local men and resources to achieve their aims. Using subterfuge and perfidy they made the local people fight and destroy their own countrymen with their own indigenous resources and reaped the benefits thereof. The beauty is that the ruse was so subtle, well painted and designed that the natives did not fight or blame the English but collaborated with them against their own fellow citizens; they tried to settle scores with their own people. Besides the methods mentioned above the English used the policy of divide and rule, carrot and stick, exemplary punishment and ruthless suppression and persecution where needed.

We must recognize the truth that Indians are adept at producing hordes of traitors who revel in their country's ruin. It is said that no race can be corrupted unless corruption is in their blood; their inherent nature. Indians' corrupt nature has meant limited warfare on the subcontinent. In India fighting wasn't needed, bribing was enough to see off armies. Every victory of the foreign invaders was facilitated by the local collaborators who betrayed their kings for some devious reward or for settling personal grievances. It is striking how little Indians have actually fought compared to ancient Greece and modern Europe.

When the English came to Punjab, they hoped for a cake walk and expected to see the same kind of warfare as they had seen in the rest of India. The Sikh soldiers were badly let down and fooled by their treacherous commanders. But despite being leaderless, disadvantaged, handicapped and deceived from the very beginning, the Sikh soldier was made of different stuff. He was a bellicose and intrepid warrior with an innate love of war and gave the British good run for their money.

Having conquered the entire land and achieved what they wanted they exploited their subjects and made them dance to their tune at their own sweet will and wish. After the First Anglo Sikh War (December 1845 - February 1846) the British took over Punjab and installed a caretaker government. The Sikh Kingdom was weakened by depriving it of precious territory and drastically reducing its army. The British were keen to get rid of the volatile Sikh threat to their empire and felt that the best strategy for this was to stick with Raja Gulab Singh. Eventually Raja Gulab Singh was invited by the Governor General at a camp on 15 March 1846. Following this Raja Gulab Singh was bestowed with the title of a

Maharaja and the Treaty of Amritsar was signed between the British and Maharaja Gulab Singh on 16 March 1846. As a result of this treaty Maharaja Gulab Singh found himself in possession of the State of Jammu and Kashmir. The Treaty of Amritsar marked the beginning of Dogra rule in Kashmir, which was to end in 1948 after an attack by the Pakistani army that led to Indo-Pakistan War of 1947. Lord Hardinge gave the following reason for the transfer of Jammu and Kashmir to Maharaja Gulab Singh, **"It was necessary last March to weaken the Sikhs by depriving them of Kashmir"**.

Having dispossessed the Sikhs of political power after the Second Anglo Sikh War in February 1849, the British tried to break their morale. They used Machiavellian methods, intimidation, exploitation, cruelty, double talk and all sort of other unethical means to undermine the self-esteem, spirit and will of the Sikhs. The leading *sardars* were either exiled or imprisoned. Their lands and properties were confiscated, and their forts and mansions were razed to the ground. The Sikh leaders were reduced to nonentities to be humiliated and ridiculed by those who, while in their (Sikh) service, had betrayed the cause of the Punjab and had now been rewarded and raised to positions of authority by the new rulers of the land.

The attitude of the people of Malwa (cis-Sutlej Sikh states) during the Anglo-Sikh wars (conflict between their trans-Sutlej brethren and the British) deserves attention. Of the innumerable Sikh chiefs of this region, only four – Patiala, Jind, Faridkot, and Chachrauli – gave unstinted support to the enemy; others either stayed on the fence or expressed sympathy with the Durbar. These included **Nabha, Ladwa, Allowal, Malaudh, Thanesar, Rupar, Kheri, Mani Majra, Shahabad, Shamgarh, Bhuria, and the Sodhis of Anandpur**. Of the two Muslim chiefs, Malerkotla sided with the

British; Mamdot, despite the offer of confirmation of his state, allowed his brother to lead his contingent against the British at Ferozeshahr. The attitude of the common people was uniformly hostile to the *feringhee*. Peasants refused to sell grain or fodder to the British army.

On the termination of the Sutlej campaign, the British government **confiscated Rupar, Ladwa, and Allowal**, took a quarter of Nabha territory and distributed it among the collaborating chiefs. The Malwa *jagirdars* were deprived of judicial powers and left only with the right to collect revenue.

MAHARAJA DULEEP SINGH (DALIP SINGH) – (4 September – 22 October 1893)

Later in life he was nicknamed 'The Black Prince of Perthshire.' He was Maharaja Ranjit Singh's youngest son and the last Maharaja of the Sikh Empire. His mother was Maharani Jind Kaur and he was her only child. After the assassination of four of his predecessors, he came to power in September 1843, at the age of five.

For a while his mother ruled, as Regent, but in December 1846 (Treaty of Bharowal), after the First Anglo- Sikh War, she was replaced by a British Resident and imprisoned. Mother and son were not allowed to meet again for thirteen and a half years (1848-1861). In April 1849 ten-year-old Duleep was placed under the care of Dr John Login and taken to Fatehgarh in U.P. Here, under Christian influences he was converted to Christianity. He was baptized on 08 March 1853 and presented with the *'Divine book of the Lord'* by Lord Dalhousie instead of the temporal kingdom of the Punjab of which he had been deprived. A copy of the Bible was the price of the Sikh Empire. Duleep Singh was the first Indian prince to be converted to Christianity. He was deposed and exiled to Britain. He sailed for England on 19 April 1854 at the age of 15, never to see the land of his birth again. In England, he became a great favourite of Queen Victoria who was godmother to several of his children.

This is perhaps the first instant on record in which a guardian has visited his own misdeeds upon his ward. The British Government was the self-constituted guardian of the Rajah, and the regent of his kingdom, a rebellion was provoked by the agents of the guardian. It was acknowledged by the guardian to be a rebellion against the government of his ward and the guardian punished that ward by confiscating his domains and his diamonds to his own use. (John Sullivan in *Are We Bound by Our Treaties?*)

He came to India twice for short sojourns. The British decided that his ailing mother was no longer a threat and she was allowed to join her son on 16 January 1861 at Spence's Hotel in Calcutta and return with him to the United Kingdom. For the second time he came in 1864 to perform the last rites of his mother, Maharani Jind Kaur who passed away in Kensington, England on 01 August 1863, at the age of 46. Since he was not granted permission to proceed to the Punjab Maharani Jind Kaur's body was cremated on the banks of River Godavari. The ashes were scattered in the river and a small memorial (Samadhi) containing a part of the ashes was erected on the left bank of the river Godavari. In 1924, Maharani Jind Kaur's granddaughter Princess Bamba Sutherland carried the urn containing her ashes from Bombay (Mumbai) to Lahore and deposited it at the "Samadhi" of Ranjit Singh, fulfilling the last wish of her grandmother.

Duleep Singh married twice, first to **Bamba Muller** (1848-18 September 1887), a Coptic Christian, on 7 June 1864 and then to **Ada Douglas Wetherill** (1868-1930) in June 1889. He had eight children in all, six (three sons and three daughters) from his first marriage to Bamba (meaning pink in Arabic) and two daughters from the second marriage. His first wife was 10 years younger than him and the second, who had been his mistress before marriage, was less than half his age.

Duleep Singh lived beyond his means; his dissipated and indulgent living led him into heavy debt. Financial difficulties rendered him desperate. By this time, he had realized that the British had deceived him and snatched away the Sikh Empire from him. Frustration and disgust made him agitate against the English for the restoration of his lost kingdom. First, he appealed to the British government and then to the Privy Council. When this did not work, he tried to interest the European powers and visited Paris and Russia. He described himself as 'England's Proud Implacable Foe.' On his way to India, he was arrested at Eden and not allowed to proceed further. In Eden, on 25 May 1886, he returned to the faith of his ancestors. A lot of importance is given to his reconversion to the Sikh religion by Sikh historians, but it really did not mean much, because he carried on in his old ways, in the ambience of the land where he perforce had to live. The bout of megalomania lasted till he realized that no one really took him seriously. He then went apologizing all around. In 1890, Duleep Singh's debts were paid and he was granted the Queen's pardon. He died on 22 October 1893, of paralysis, at the age of 55 years. The funeral took place on 29 October in the little church opposite the house of his (seventeen thousand acres) sporting estate at Elveden and he was buried at Elvedon in Suffolk (England) beside the graves of his first wife Bamba and son Edward. The last of Duleep Singh's surviving children, his eldest daughter Princess Bamba Sutherland died at Lahore on 10 March 1957, at the age of 89. So far as the record shows, there are no living direct descendants of Maharaja Duleep Singh. Maharaja Duleep Singh was the squire (a country noble man) of Elveden and after his death, the estate at Elveden was sold by the Maharaja's trustees at the India Office to the 1st Earl of Iveagh for pounds 1,59,000. The estate is owned today by the present Lord Iveagh.

MUTINY OF 1857

The mutiny lacked an all-India character and, also had a considerable absence of leadership. The inability of finding a person upon whom to bestow the leadership which was indispensable for organizing such a movement proved to be a vital cause for the failure of the mutiny. The Indian response therefore largely grew out of local compulsions and immediate petty interests and historical exigencies. Economic grievances had been the bone of contention, but religion provided the necessary tinder to spark a popular uprising across the nation against the fatal features of an authoritarian regime.

For some time, the rising appeared to be a national revolt against a usurping foreigner. However very soon it became clear that there was very little in common between the two allies fighting the English. The Muslim sought the restoration of Muslim rule; the Hindu hoped to put the Marathas back in to power. The two communities were only united to the extent that they were fighting a common enemy, the English. The situation in Punjab was different from that which prevailed in the rest of India. The sepoy and the people in Punjab were disaffected. Punjabi Mussalmans turned a deaf ear to their Hindustani co-religionists' exhortation to *jihad* against the pig-eating despoilers of Islam. Punjabi Hindus and, with greater reason, the Sikhs refused to listen to the belated appeal to save Hindu *dharma* from beef-eating foreigners who used cow fat to grease their cartridges. This was expected because **the enemy of yesterday was posing as today's friend for ulterior motives**. Indian historians write that the Sikhs sided with the British during the 1857 mutiny (which is a fact), but no where do they mention the reason why and the atrocities committed by the native troops on the Sikhs and Punjabis during the Anglo-Sikh wars and the treatment they meted out to them after the wars. Why did they not join the Sikhs/Punjabis against the British? Now the only people who could save the English were the Punjabis. And of the Punjabis, the only ones who could be expected to turn a deaf ear to appeals to restore Mughal or Maratha rule were the Sikhs. The British fully exploited Sikh animosity towards Hindustani Hindus and Mussalmans. It is true that the Sikhs did not join the mutiny and some reasons are as follows:

- The Sikhs had not been taken into confidence. They had neither been consulted nor invited.

- The Sikhs, who might well have gambled with the chance of recovering power, were leaderless. Their king, Maharaja Duleep Singh had renounced Sikhism and converted to Christianity, he had thus forsaken them. The other leaders were either dead or living in exile under strict British surveillance.

- The Sikhs could not volunteer to help the erstwhile enemies of their country. The wounds of the Anglo Sikh Wars that were fought just eight years ago were still fresh in their memories. The *purabiahs* had helped the British destroy the independent kingdom of Punjab in 1845-46 and reduce it to British subjection in 1848-49. This was not surprising because those, who in the summer of 1857 claimed to be crusaders for freedom, were the very people who eight years earlier had been the *feringhees*' instruments in reducing the Punjabis to servitude.

- The behavior of the *purabiah* soldiers during the war and during and after the annexation of the Punjab had been haughty and insulting. It had caused deep wounds in the hearts of the Sikh people. They had an ill will towards the Hindustani sepoy (*purabiah*), who disdained to mix with the Sikhs as men of low caste. The Khalsa had held the Hindustani in extreme contempt; it thus widened the breach between the Punjabi and the Hindustani and rendered any coalition the more difficult.

- Since the Meerut and Delhi mutineers had proclaimed the restoration of Mughal rule, Sikhs who had been brought up on tales of Mughal atrocities against their forefathers reacted sharply to Bahadur Shah's proclamation. For evident reasons, the Sikhs could not espouse the cause of the Mughal emperor, Bahadur Shah (1837-1862), whom the mutineers had raised to the throne. For **over two centuries the Sikhs had fought against Mughal tyranny** and they could not now in anyway be persuaded to support an alliance which might have resulted in its re-establishment. (Sikh soldiers were in the van of the assault on Delhi. In the security provided by the Sikhs, the British officer Major Hodson ignored the presence of an armed mob of several thousand, stripped the three Mughal princes naked and shot them with his carbine. Sikhs took the corpses of the princes to Chandni Chowk and laid them out for display in front of Gurdwara Sis Ganj, where 182 years earlier their guru, Tegh Bahadur, had been executed by the orders of Emperor Aurangzeb).

After the mutiny, the administration of India was directly taken over by the British crown. The Governor-General of India now came to be called the Viceroy of India. Jammu and Kashmir had already been segregated from Punjab in 1846 (it was sold to Maharaja Gulab Singh). In the administrative change after the mutiny, Haryana and Delhi were added to the Punjab province. Most of Haryana was a desert and deficient in food, the people spoke a different language and their way of life and values were different from the Punjabis. Delhi was a commercial city in contrast to pastoral Punjab. These mismatches created problems for future governments.

Though the mutiny of 1857 could not bring forth an immediate political victory, it eventually prepared ground for a long-drawn struggle against the British leading to its logical culmination. Thus, out of the mutiny was born the Indian Freedom Movement. It was during this struggle after the mutiny that the Sikhs were drawn into it and their sacrifices were much more than any other community. Their contribution was tremendous, commensurate to their total population

CRESCAT E FLUVIIS (Strength from the waters – the motto of the Punjab).

Ten years of anarchy, two sanguine wars and lack of leadership deprived the Sikhs of the will to resist the annexation of their kingdom. The British sensed that what Punjab required was an autocratic government with good administration and justice. The British followed a programme of public works by building roads, railways, schools and hospitals. The greatest of these public undertakings was the digging of canals and reclamation of desert lands in the *doabs* (land between two rivers) between the Punjab Rivers. This work temporarily came to a halt during the mutiny but was resumed soon after. The land produced far in excess of the government revenue investment for building the canals and Punjab became the granary of India. Special grants were made to set up stud farms for army horses and mules and later for select breeds of cattle.

The Sikhs had been chosen to rehabilitate and colonize many of these barren wastes. The area specially chosen for them was a *bar* (tract i.e., large area of land) known as *nili bar*, irrigated by the Chenab Canal. With the prosperity ushered in by the colonization scheme the land prices escalated and the Punjabis became the most prosperous peasantry of India; and, of the Punjabis, the Sikhs became the most thriving of all. The government and the peasants reaped extraordinary profits and it is not surprising that the Sikhs soon forgot the past and became the staunchest supporters of the Raj.

The prosperity and the preference shown towards the Sikhs in recruitment to the army had an important bearing on the future and the caste complex of the community. The economic advantages of being Sikh checked the disintegration of Sikhism and its lapse into Hinduism. There was a phenomenal rise in the number of Sikhs during the last decade of the 19th century and the first decade of the 20th century. This was due largely to the patronage of the government, which had posts reserved exclusively for *keshdhari* (with hair) Sikhs in the army and later in the civilian services. Thus, the gloomy prediction of Lord Dalhousie of the possibility of the disappearance of the Sikhs was averted by his own policies augmented by his high-ranking staff in the army and the administration.

RELIGIOUS MOVEMENTS The three religious movements namely the Nirankari, Namdhari and Radha Soami that came into being after the Punjab was annexed by the British and later the **Singh Sabha and Social Reform** (Sikh Renaissance) Movement have been adequately covered in Volume 1.

CHAPTER- 3

SIKH AWAKENING AND STRUGGLE FOR THEIR RIGHTS

RURAL INDEBTEDNESS, COLONIAL BILL AND PEASANT AGITATION

The development of the canal colonies brought in an era of prosperity that Punjab had never seen before. But this prosperity brought in its wake other economic changes which radically altered the social fabric of life. The halcyon days soon came to an end. The 1870's ushered in a period of peasant indebtedness which had never been known in the country before. The reasons for this were:

- The increase in earnings from agriculture also saw the increase in land prices. It rose from mere Rs 10/- per acre in 1870 to more than Rs 100/- per acre by the turn of the century. It was Rs 438 per acre in 1925 and touched Rs 477 per acre in 1933-34. Small farmers were unable to resist the temptation to sell their holdings. Thus, the number of landless farmers assumed alarming proportions.

- The famine of 1869, a cattle epidemic in 1877 and failure of five out of six harvests in 1919-21 took a heavy toll of lives of cattle that further accentuated the problems of the farmer. The farmer was unable to pay revenue due from him and was compelled to borrow.

- The elaborate legal system introduced by the British contributed to the impoverishment of the agriculturists and the enrichment of moneylenders and lawyers.

- The peasantry (the Jat Sikh in particular) reverted to their traditional habit of drowning sorrow in drink and opium (in some districts). This led to an increase in crime. In addition, there were family feuds and altercations concerning the use of canal water which were common to all agricultural communities, but the Jat Sikh indulged in violence without motive or provocation and had to borrow money to defend him in court.

- Inordinate expenses at weddings for feasting and dowries for daughters and the cost of buying wives in some districts where there was acute shortage of women due to female infanticide.

- Some natural causes such as the increase of population led to immense pressure on land and holdings were fragmented. The land holdings shrunk in size and became uneconomical.

Punjabi peasants proved to be more quarrelsome and litigious than any other people of India. Forty percent of the adult population of the province attended law courts as parties or witnesses and spent 3.4 crores of rupees in litigation every year.

The Punjab Land Alienation Act, 1900

The Act was designed to protect the agriculturists from the clutches of the moneylenders. It succeeded in safeguarding the interests of cultivators; but it also sowed the seeds of racial separatism. The question of who was or was not an agriculturist was not decided by actual occupation but by caste. The act severed the links between the agriculturists (Jats, Rajputs and scheduled castes) and non-agriculturists (Khatris, Aroras and Banias) and put them in opposing camps. It affected the Sikhs the most because caste considerations mattered little among Muslims and were rigid among the Hindus. Sikhs had gone a long way in breaking the barriers of caste, but due to the Land Alienation Act, economic and political interests the differences resurfaced and got reflected in social life as well. The Sikh community split into three racial divisions the Jats, the non-Jats (Brahmins, Kshatriyas, and Vaishyas) and the untouchables (Mazhabis, Ramdasias, Sikligahrs, Kabir panthis. etc.). All three found that they had more in common with their own caste irrespective of religion and preferred to interact and marry into their own caste Hindu families rather than families of their own co-religionists from other castes.

The Land Alienation Act saved agriculture land from passing to money lenders but did not solve the problem of rural indebtedness. Famines and series of calamities ravaged the Punjab and an epidemic of bubonic plague took a toll of over four million lives. The administration remained insensitive to these disasters and continued to increase revenue instead of remitting it. Harsh punishment was inflicted on defaulters. The introduction of the **Colonial Bill** added fuel to fire, and it became the immediate cause of unrest. The most objectionable part of the bill was that it made land the property of the government and the farmer a mere tenant. It restricted the rights of colonisers to make wills and denied them the right to cut trees on their land. The bill made the government both landlord and administrator and enhanced the rights of the administration at the expense of the distressed tenant. It also deprived the tenant of the protection of the civil courts. While the discontent over the **Colonial Bill** was still brewing, a new settlement of Rawalpindi district was made at a higher rate of assessment, and the charge on water from the Bari Doab Canals was increased. The districts of Lyallpur (mainly colonised by Sikhs) and Rawalpindi were most affected by these measures.

There were protests, agitations, forceful criticism by the Indian press and vigorous opposition by the Indian members of Punjab Legislative Council. Punjab was becoming fertile soil for revolutionary seed. The stirring song ***Pagri Sambhal O Jatta*** by Banke Dayal became popular. These measures of the authorities caused uneasiness among Sikh soldiers, many of whom had relatives in the colonies. The government realised the danger of having a disgruntled peasantry and particularly a peasantry from which it drew the largest number of recruits for the army and on whose loyalty depended the internal security of the country. The authorities relented when they realised that the measures adopted would cause trouble in times to come. They managed to wriggle out of the precarious situation. The governor general, Lord Minto, vetoed the bill and the land tax and water rates were rolled back.

SIKH EMIGRATION, POLITICAL MOVEMENTS AND COMMUNISM

The prosperity and euphoria produced by the canal colonies, patronage in the services and introduction of western system of education was short-lived, however it produced economic, social, and political changes in the Sikh community. Driven by economic conditions, in the early years of the twentieth century, families which could somehow afford or raise money sent their younger sons to explore other avenues of employment or to seek their fortunes in foreign lands. Sikh communities sprang up in Myanmar (Burma), Malaya, Singapore, Thailand, Cambodia, the Philippines, China and the Asian coast. At the same time small entrepreneurs set up business in countries on the eastern coast of Africa.

A small number of the more enterprising Sikhs ventured across the Pacific to Canada and the United States. The first Sikh migrants to Canada settled in British Columbia and later those who went to United States settled in California. On the American continent emigrants had to face racial discrimination. They were paid lower wages than the white workers; there was anti-Asian feeling among Canadians, assaults on Sikhs and from 1907 onwards several enactments were passed by the British Columbia's state legislature to check Indian (90% were Sikhs) immigration and prohibit employment of Indians in certain places. In 1908 the Canadian Government passed two orders-in-council to deal with the ingress of Indian nationals. Firstly, it raised the sum of money required to be in the possession of an intended immigrant from $25 to $200; and secondly it authorised the minister of the interior to prohibit entry of travellers unless they came "from the country of their birth or citizenship by a continuous journey, and on through tickets purchased before leaving their country of birth or citizenship." Both these orders were specifically directed against the Indians. Chinese and Japanese immigrants were exempted from these orders. The "continuous passage" regulation was more pointedly aimed at the Indians as it was known that no company ran ships directly from India to Canada and India had no ships of her own.

The fact that Sikh immigrants were British subjects created legal complications for the Canadian Government. Therefore, British Columbian legislation (Vancouver) required the sanction of the Federal Government (Ottawa) and the Federal Government had to consult the government of United Kingdom (London), which in turn had to watch the reaction of the Government of India (Calcutta now Kolkata). All of them were in agreement that British Columbians had every right to exclude Indian immigrants; their only concern was that measures should be so framed that no suspicion of racial discrimination should be discernible. **The enactments passed were invalidated by the courts**.

In 1908, Mr Kenzie King (later prime minister of Canada) visited London and Kolkata in order to stop immigration at source. The orders-in-council were made substantive law by amending the existing act and then incorporating all the prohibitory clauses in the Immigration Act of 1910. The Immigration Act of 1910 came up for scrutiny before the Canadian Supreme Court in 1913, when a group of 39 Indians (mostly Sikhs) landed in British Columbia by a Japanese ship, the *Panama Maru*. They succeeded in obtaining writ of *habeas corpus* (a written order that an arrested person be brought before a judge or into court for decision) against the Immigration Department's order of deportation. Within a fortnight of the passing of the judgment, the Canadian Government promulgated a new order-in-council forbidding entry at any port of British Columbia. A month later, "the continuous passage" and the $200 clauses were reintroduced through new orders-in-council carefully worded to circumvent the verdict of the Supreme Court. The door to Canada was now firmly shut with a notice outside printed in invisible ink reading "**Indians Keep Out**."

Sikh immigration to the United States was a spill-over from Canada. As the Canadian Immigration Department became stricter, the number of immigrants to the States increased. American whites, however, reacted even more violently than the Canadians. In 1908 there were pogroms against Orientals by an organisation known as the Asiatic Exclusion League in order to stop their immigration. Whenever there was a lull in racial violence, immigration would restart and by the end of 1910 there were about 6000 Sikhs in California. In an era of apartheid, the United States did not bother with legal niceties; Indians were sent back for one or the other of three reasons: "liable to pubic charge," "suffering from dangerous contagious disease," or "violates alien contract labour laws." The local press also whipped up racial hatred against the "**turbaned tide**" and the "**ragheads**." Those who had succeeded in immigrating had to face constant harassment from the police and whites. Thus, the doors of the United States were also slammed in the face of the Sikhs.

This racial discrimination and maltreatment in turn developed a xenophobia which provided fertile ground for the dissemination of Marxism. This xenophobic Marxism manifested itself in the formation of the Gadhar Party by the immigrants. The party began disseminating literature to Sikhs all over the world and organising revolutionary activities. In India too, several factors that comprised mainly of ill-treatment and repression of Sikhs created resentment against British rule. This further resulted in the emergence of three political parties: the Communists, the Nationalists, and the Akalis. In the years following the First World War, when steps were taken to increase people's participation in administration, these political parties vied for power. No doubt the Akalis were the most influential of the three.

THE GHADR PARTY

A party known as the Hindustani Workers of the Pacific Coast was formed at Stockton (U. S.) on 02 June 1913. Sohan Singh of Bhakna (Amritsar) and Hardyal were elected president and secretary. Jwala Singh (a prosperous rancher of Stockton known as the "potato king") remained behind the scene but provided most of the funds, including scholarships for Indian students. The party bought premises in San Francisco and started publishing its official organ, called *Ghadr* (revolution) on 01 November 1913 in Urdu and later many other Indian languages - the largest issue being in *Gurmukhi*. Within a few months, the *Ghadr* began to circulate among Indian communities in many other countries. Thousands of copies were sent to India. Thereafter the organisation also came to be known as the Ghadr party whose main objective was to free India from the British yoke and establish a *Panchayati raj*

(Republican state). **The Komagata Maru incident** took place in May 1914. This further agitated the immigrants.

Since the war in Europe was in the offing and Canada was a part of the British Empire, the Ghadr party shifted their revolutionary activities to the United States. A week after the war was declared, a large number of men including Jwala Singh (he led the first band but was arrested at Calcutta) and Sohan Singh Bhakna volunteered and enlisted for revolutionary service in India; Hardyal, who had been arrested earlier escaped to Switzerland. Thus, devoid of a leader the control of the party in California fell to a dishonest man **Ram Chandra**, a Brahmin from Peshawar. Ghadrites continued to pour into India, in batches from Canada, United States and many other countries with Indian population. **Ajit Singh** and **Kartar Singh Saraba** (1896-1915 - hanged on 16 Nov. 1915) were prominent figures among the revolutionaries. But alas! The Ghadr party had not taken pains to study the situation in India. The atmosphere was far from conducive for revolution. Everything in India was oriented towards the war effort. There was very little that the Ghadr party could achieve as compared to the efforts put in.

The *Ghadr* men used Japanese vessels to travel. The party carried out propaganda in Japan where Maulvi Barkat Ullah was a professor in Tokyo University. Later he came to San Francisco and his presence attracted many Muslims to the party. In February 1915 a rising in a Muslim unit (5th Light Infantry – the "loyal Fifth") in Singapore was successfully instigated but the mutiny was soon quelled. Indian revolutionaries were active in London, Paris and Berlin for at least a decade before the formation of the Ghadr party. However, when the war broke out, they all shifted their activities to Berlin. Hardayal arrived in Germany in the spring of 1914 and apprised his countrymen of the Ghadr party (by then it had nearly 10,000 active members). The "Berlin-India" committee succeeded in persuading the German foreign minister, Zimmerman to provide funds and arms to the *Ghadrites*.

German participation created factions in the Ghadr party. The rank and file were constituted by the Sikh workers and peasants. Ram Chandra, who had little rapport with the Sikhs, had acquired over-all control of the party. The nominee of the "Berlin-India" Committee, Haramba Lal Gupta had German money in his pockets. Misunderstandings arose between the rival Indian groups and between the Indians and the Germans. Two attempts to smuggle arms to India by the Germans failed. In February 1916 the "Berlin-India Committee," with the approval of the German foreign office, sent out a Bengali, Dr Chandra Kant Chakravarty, to take over the conduct of the Ghadr movement and furnished him with large sums of money. Chakravarty appropriated the money to his own use and fed the Germans with imaginary reports. When the Germans discovered the truth, they washed their hands of the Ghadr party.

Chakravarty walked away with most of the money given by the Germans. Ram Chandra and his friends (a group almost entirely of Hindus) had control of the donations made by the immigrants, the party journal, and the headquarters. The illiterate rank and file (entirely Sikh), who had staked everything including their lives were left with nothing. Thus, religious differences further accentuated the rift. The United States police arrested 17 Indian revolutionaries along with 18 Germans. The trial of the accused persons ended on a dramatic note. On the last day one of the accused (Ram Singh - a rich Sikh landowner who had given thousands of dollars to the Ghadr cause - thousands of dollars which were turned over to Ram Chandra) whipped out a revolver and shot Ram Chandra. The assailant was in turn shot dead by the marshal of the court. Special tribunals at Lahore and other parts of

India and abroad tried and convicted several hundreds of revolutionaries. Sentences ranging from hanging to long terms of imprisonment were given. Besides these, many soldiers were court-martialed and shot dead.

Though the Ghadr rebellion was suppressed, it continued to ferment and erupted in the form of Akali terrorists known as *Babbars* during the Akali Agitation. The *Babbars* were largely recruited from the remnants of the Ghadr organisation. The conversion of the Ghadrites to communism came after the war. Bolshevik agents made contact with the Ghadr party in America and Canada. For the relief of political sufferers and the spread of communism, funds were liberally supplied by Canadian–American Ghadrites and Moscow. Communist infiltration split the Ghadr party. The majority of *Ghadrites* either turned anti-communist or were submerged by the wave of anti-communism. Their quarrels often led to violence and these disputes carried on till India's independence. In 1948, the assets of the Ghadr party were turned over to the Indian ambassador in the US, thus bringing to an end its 30-year-old journey.

The Ghadr rebellion failed for a variety of reasons: lack of arms; lack of experience; lack of education (most of the workers were illiterate-only 2% of them knew Urdu or Punjabi); bad leadership; lack of intelligence and security of plans; tension between the Germans and *Ghadrites*; high quality and efficient British Intelligence service; stern measures taken by the Government of India and brutal methods adopted by the Punjab police. Above all it failed because the masses of Punjab were not ready for it.

The aim of the Ghadr movement was not achieved and nor did it pose a very serious threat to the British Raj. Nevertheless, it is of considerable importance to the historian and it had its effects. It was the first secular movement which aimed to liberate India using arms. The Ghadr party attracted Hindus and Muslims into its fold and invited and made contacts with terrorist organisations in other parts of the country. It brought about a radical change in the political outlook of the Sikhs. It marked the beginning of the end of three quarters of a century of unquestioned loyalty to the British Raj.

THE KOMAGATA MARU

Indian immigrants to Canada in those days were subjected to many humiliating restrictions (the continuous passage and the $200 clauses for emigration, racial discrimination, less wages, racial violence etc.). In order to comply with the requirements of the Canadian government and primarily to circumvent the continuous passage bill, Baba Gurdit Singh (1860-1954), a prosperous businessman of Singapore chartered a Japanese passenger ship, Komagata Maru (aka Guru Nanak Jahaz) for six months.

Aboard this vessel were 376 Indians (of whom all but 30 were Sikhs) collected from Calcutta (now Kolkata-India) and ports *en route*. On 23 May 1914, the ship docked in Vancouver harbour. When the ship moored (dropped anchor), it was cordoned off and only 22 men who could prove their Canadian domicile were allowed to land. The rest were told to go back. After an almost two-month standoff, when all humanitarian (appeals to the Canadian people and government, the King of England, the Duke of Connaught, the Viceroy and Indian leaders), socio-political (feisty demonstrations by ethnic Indians on Vancouver's shores), economic (the Sikh labourers in Canada raised $22,000 to pay for the Charter) and legal (Vancouver Sikhs took the case of the Komagata Maru to court) efforts failed, the ship was eventually turned away. The Komagata Maru set sail again on its return voyage. None of her passengers was allowed to disembark *en route* (several of the travellers had their homes in Hong Kong and Singapore).

Finally, the Komagata Maru arrived at Budge-Budge harbour at the mouth of the river Hoogly in India, on 26 September 1914. It was searched by the police and the passengers were not allowed to go to Calcutta. They were all ordered to board a special train kept ready for them to be taken to the Punjab. War had broken out while the Komagata Maru was still at sea, and the government had empowered itself with the right to restrict the liberty of returning emigrants. The Sikhs refused to obey and left the ship in a procession, carrying the Guru Granth Sahib in their midst. In the tumult a shot was fired and subsequently the police opened fire, killing 18 men and wounding another 25 (including the 9-year-old son of Baba Gurdit Singh). Gurdit Singh and 28 of his companions escaped. The rest were rounded up, sent to Punjab and lodged in different jails. A month later, on 28 October, 173 passengers, mostly Sikhs arriving at Kolkata from America and South-east Asian countries by the vessel *Tasu Maru* were similarly interned in the Central jails of Montgomery and Multan. This gave a powerful stimulus to the anti-British and *Ghadar* propaganda in India.

A trail of violence followed the departure of the Komagata Maru. In Vancouver, the services of a Eurasian policeman, William Hopkinson, were hired to break up the *Ghadr* organisation. Hopkinson's chief aide was a man called Bela Singh and they let loose a reign of terror. Two of Bela Singh's henchmen were found murdered, so he retaliated by killing two and wounding six other men in the gurdwara, during their post-funeral service. As a result of the prevailing tyranny, Hopkinson was shot dead by Mewa Singh, the priest of a gurdwara, on 21 October 1914. Mewa Singh in turn was sentenced to death and hanged on 11 January 1915. Every year, the Sikhs of Canada and America celebrate the anniversary of Mewa Singh's martyrdom. Bela Singh who had fled Vancouver after murdering and betraying his co-religionists was hacked to pieces in his village Jaina by the Babbar Akalis (immortal lions) in 1933.

Today there are memorials dedicated to the Komagata Maru incident at Budge-Budge and Vancouver. More than a century later, on Wednesday the 18th May 2016 the Canadian Prime Minister issued a formal apology in his country's House of Commons for the 1914 Komagata Maru incident. The incident is a reminder, particularly for Canada's considerable Sikh population, of the widespread discrimination and bigotry meted out to Indians and other Asians on the west coast of America a century ago.

RIKAB GANJ AGITATION (1913-1920)

In May 1913 when the new capital of India at New Delhi was being built, the government acquired land attached to gurdwara Rikab Ganj (the sacred site where Guru Tegh Bahadur's headless body was cremated in 1675) in Delhi for a sum of Rs 39,133/- and demolished the old boundary wall. The land was required to suit the plan of the new Viceregal Lodge. The Sikhs challenged the mahant's (priests, custodians or care takers who were Hindus as often as Sikhs) right to alienate gurdwara property and condemned the demolition as sacrilegious. The agitation that was launched had to be postponed due to the 1914-1918 war. It was, however, taken up again after the war. As the government refused to respect Sikh sentiment, the Sikhs decided to launch a *morcha* (battle front) and send in *Shahidi jathas* (suicide squads of martyrs). An advertisement in a Sikh newspaper *Akali* published from Lahore invited one hundred men who should be willing to sacrifice their lives. There was an overwhelming response and within a fortnight, seven hundred volunteers, including some Hindus and Muslims, had offered to join the *Shahidi jatha*. The government realised its folly and the seriousness of the situation. Before the *jathas* could arrive, the wall was reconstructed by Maharaja Ripudaman Singh of Nabha on behalf of the Government of India, and the acquired land was restored to a committee of representative Sikhs who had taken over the management of the gurdwara. When the wall was built, the government had its photograph published in newspapers.

THE JALLIANWALA BAGH MASSACRE (SUNDAY 13 APRIL 1919)

The Jallianwala Bagh in Amritsar, literally a garden belonging to the Jallas, derives its name from that of the owners of the place in Sikh times. It was then the property of the family of Sardar Himmat Singh (d. 1829), a nobleman in the court of Maharaja Ranjit Singh (1780-1839), who came from village Jalla, now in Fatehgarh Sahib District of Punjab. The family was collectively known as Jallhewala or simply Jallhe or Jalle. The Bagh, once a garden or garden house, was at the time of the massacre in 1919, an uneven and unoccupied irregular quadrangular plot of land, approximately 225 X 180 meters. It had an asymmetrical wall around it that varied vastly in height, size and construction. There was only one ingress and egress.

On 10 April 1919 half a dozen people were killed and another 30 wounded during the protests against the Rowalatt Act. The angry mob got out of hand and in the rampage set fire to government property and began to assault white people. In this riot five Englishmen were killed and a missionary Miss Marcella Sherwood severely assaulted. The army was called in. Brigadier General Reginald Edward Harry Dyer (09 October 1864 - 24 July 1927), commander 45 Infantry Brigade, marched from Jullundur to Amritsar with Gorkha troops and armoured cars and arrived in Amritsar in the evening on 11 April. The next afternoon i.e., 12 April, he marched his troops through the bazaars and in the evening, he received news of vandalism. The general proclaimed a state of emergency and declared all meetings illegal (majority of the citizens were unaware of this declaration). Meanwhile, the local Congress had already announced a meeting at Jallianwala Bagh at 4.30 pm for the *Baisakhi* fair on 13 April.

From the early hours of the morning on 13 April, a large number of people mostly Sikhs, had poured into the city from the surrounding villages for the *Baisakhi* festival (first of *Baisakh* being the birth anniversary of the Khalsa). These Sikhs, ignorant of the announcement went to the nearby Bagh to pass time till it was cool enough to return home. For the Sikh villagers (mostly illiterate) it was just another diversion, a *tamasa*. The total number of people in Jallianwala Bagh was estimated at between 15 and 20 thousand, Sikhs comprising a large portion of them. As soon as Brigadier Dyer received news of the meeting, he marched a platoon of infantry to Jallianwala and on reaching there at about 5.15 pm; he occupied the only entrance/exit to the Bagh and without giving any warning to the crowd to disperse, opened fire on them with .303 rifles. The firing lasted for about 20 minutes, in which 1650 rounds of ammunition were fired. The official figures of the causalities were 379 killed and 1200 wounded, whereas the unofficial figures were much more. Brigadier Dyer imposed a curfew in the city and returned to his camp leaving the dying with the dead without any possibility of help reaching them. Hundreds of unarmed, defenseless Indians had been murdered in cold blood by a senior British military officer, in the heart of Amritsar, the holiest city of the Sikhs, on a day sacred to them. It was indeed a **black Sunday**. When the news was conveyed to **Sir Michael O'Dwyer** (1864-1940), the Lieutenant Governor of Punjab, he fully approved of the action.

Martial Law was clamped in Punjab. After Jallianwala, the agitations and demonstrations all over the province of Punjab took a very ugly turn. There was arson, looting, riots, rampage and assaults all over. The army administrator Brigadier General Dyer had Amritsar city's water and electric supply cut; in the street where the missionary lady had been assaulted, he made Indian passers-by crawl on their bellies; specially constituted courts tried and summarily sentenced people to death and terms of imprisonment. All over the province there was public flogging and many other humiliating atrocities committed on Indians. In the seven weeks that Punjab was administered by martial law nearly 1200 people were killed and at least 3,600 wounded. Sir Michael O'Dwyer, the man who claimed that he had saved the empire, had in fact dealt it the most grievous blow by alienating all Indians, including its staunchest supporters, the Sikhs.

"No British action, during the whole course of our history in India, has struck a severer blow to Indian faith in British justice than the massacre at Amritsar," wrote the Westminister Gazette. The sun had begun to set on the British Empire. Rabindranath Tagore renounced his British Knighthood. The Hunter Inquiry Committee (named after its chairman, Lord Hunter) held Brigadier General R.E.H. Dyer (nicknamed the Butcher of Amritsar) guilty of a mistaken notion of duty, and he was relieved of his command and prematurely retired. The general received a sum of 26,317 pounds from his English admirers who called him, 'The man who saved India'. The Jallianwala Bagh was acquired by the nation for a sum of Rs 5, 60,472/- on 21 August 1920 and today it is a memorial (the monument that was constructed after India's independence was inaugurated by Dr Rajendra Prasad, the first President of the Republic of India, on 13 April 1961). **Sir Michael O'Dwyer** was shot dead by a Sikh, **Udham Singh (26 December 1899 - 13 March 1940)**, at a public meeting in London on 13 March 1940. Udham Singh was hanged on 13 June 1940.

THE GURDWARA REFORM MOVEMENT (1920-1925) is covered in volume 1.

CHAPTER- 4

THE FREEDOM STRUGGLE

The Sikhs in the Punjab because of their past and present services and sacrifices in the cause of the Empire, occupied an important, distinct and unique position in the country, unapproached and unapproachable by any other community in India. Their influential position was partly based on historical and political factors, partly on their military prestige; and partly on their high education level and economic importance. The British had much to gain from the Sikhs, but they antagonized them badly. The leaders of Singh Sabha were loyalists and despite their chagrin remained true to their pledge and were faithful and passive to the very end. After the Jallianwala incident Brigadier General Dyer was invited to the Golden Temple and presented with a *siropa* (turban and *kirpan*). From 1914 onwards the Singh Sabha movement began to lose its popularity and credit in the eyes of the people and also its hold on the Sikh masses.

The Sikh contribution during the mutiny of 1857 and during the war effort for the First World War (1914-1918) both in men and material was bigger than that of any other community in India and yet, in spite of this they were pained to find that local government authorities continued to treat them like trash rather than war heroes. The "**Indent System**" which forced the villages to provide a certain number of recruits for the war and pressure used to raise war funds; the maltreatment of Sikh emigrants by the Canadian and American whites and the refusal of the government in India and England to help them even after repeated requests; the *Komagata Maru* incident; the treatment of the Ghadrites; the shooting at Jallianwala; **Rowlatt Act 1919** which gave extraordinary powers to the government to put any person behind bars on suspicion without any definite reason; the tyranny of the martial law regime; the atrocities committed during the gurdwara reform agitation; creation of separate electorate for Muslims followed by the Communal Award; the divide and rule policy practiced by the English; the persecution by the authorities and other factors added fuel to the smouldering fire. In this way the British alienated their staunchest supporters, the Sikhs. They tried to make amends with certain promises and actions and with the help of influential Sikhs, but it was too little and too late. The efforts were inadequate and effete. The political climate in the country had started changing with the advent of the freedom struggle and the Sikhs were drawn closer to the freedom movement. They turned their backs on the British and jumped on the bandwagon of the fight for freedom.

Constitutional Reforms and the Communal Award

Of all the provinces of British India, Punjab was the last to awaken politically and of the three communities in Punjab; the Sikhs were the biggest laggards. They lacked guidance and adequate interest.

Looking into the rise in political consciousness, the political unrest and various services rendered by Indians and other factors, the British wanted to give the Indians a greater share in governance. Thus, there was the ***Minto – Morley Reforms*** **(1909)** (named jointly after the governor–general and the secretary of state), the **Montague–Chelmsford Reforms** (named jointly after the secretary of state and the governor–general) *and the* ***Government of India Act, 1919,*** the **Simon Commission** followed the **three round table conferences** between November 1930 and December 1932 and ultimately the **Communal Award** and the **Government of India Act 1935**. The reforms provided for a separate electorate and weightage for the Muslims in the states in which they were a minority as well as at the center. Separate electorate meant that only Muslims could vote for Muslims and weightage entailed that they should be given advantage to upset the Hindu preponderance in numbers. No notice was taken of a demand by the Chief Khalsa Diwan for similar concessions to Sikhs. The Indian National Congress and the Muslim League met at Lucknow and drew up the bilateral **Lucknow Pact** (1916) between Hindus and Muslims which gave Muslims 50% of the communal seats in Punjab, but the Sikhs were not invited to these talks.

All along, the Muslims vehemently opposed joint electorates and held on tenaciously to the demand for separate communal electorates for the Muslims. They claimed that the seats in the legislatures of the Muslim majority provinces of Punjab and Bengal should be based on the actual population ratios there, while seats in provinces in which Muslims were in a minority should be based on negotiated ratios. This weighed favourably towards Muslims in the manner of the 1916 Lucknow Pact. The Sikhs (a minority of significant standing in Punjab) were not accorded strength of representation equivalent to that given to Muslims in those provinces in which the latter were in a minority. The Sikhs felt that Muslims who had been granted relatively stronger representation in the Punjab legislature than that recommended by the Simon Commission had been unduly favoured. Another point of resentment was the failure of the British government to take into account the 1.9% increase in Sikh population documented by the 1931 census. The Sikhs claimed a one-third share in all seats and appointments in Punjab as their just and fair share. The Sikhs, who formed 12% of Punjab population, received 18% representation; Muslims, who formed 11% of the population of Bihar and Orissa, received 25% representation.

A memorandum of Sikh representation drafted mostly by **Sardar Ujjal Singh** (an Arora Sikh who owned large estates in Multan district. He remained in the hub of Sikh politics till 1955 and became the governor of Punjab in 1965) was sent, which said, "While anxious to maintain their individuality as a separate community they [the Sikhs] are always ready to cooperate with their sister communities for the development of a united nation. They would, therefore, be the first to welcome a declaration that no considerations of caste or religion shall affect the matter of organisation of a national government in the country. They are prepared to stand on merit alone, provided they, in common with others, are permitted to grow unhampered by any impediments, in the way of reservation for any other community." If, however, separate representation was to continue the memorandum demanded that in the Punjab Legislature communal proportions should be fixed as follows – 40% Muslim, 30% Hindu and 30% Sikh. Claim was made for Sikh representation in Sindh (if it was made into a separate province), Delhi and the North West Frontier Province. After the Communal Award (16 April 1932) and the Government of India Act 1935 (04 August 1935), the Sikhs took various actions, however, none of these measures succeeded in persuading the British to withdraw the award or to recast its terms. Ultimately the Sikhs rejected the Communal Award. **In spite of their present and past status and services and sacrifices in the cause of the Empire, the Sikhs were everywhere in a minority and as experience had shown they would go virtually unrepresented.**

Some important and interesting reforms and events during the process of constitutional reforms (1909-1935) are listed below:

>The Act of 1919 introduced ***'Dyarchy'*** or dual form of government in the provinces. Under this system the subjects to be dealt with by the Provincial Government were divided into two parts. The "reserved subjects" (such as law and order and land revenue) were administered by the Governor with the help of his Executive council **nominated** by him while the "transferred subjects" were administered by the Governor with the help of the ministers **chosen** by him from the elected members of the Legislature. These ministers were also accountable to the Provincial Legislature. Their position was thus a very precarious one because they had to serve two masters at one and the same time. Vide the Government of India Act 1935 *Dyarchy*, which had been abolished in the provinces, was introduced in the centre. Subjects such as defense and foreign affairs were to be "reserved" and therefore the prerogative of the governor-general. Thus, the governor-general and governor still reserved all autocratic powers.

>The 1920 elections under the new Act of 1919 saw the emergence of the **Unionist Party** headed by Mian Fazl-i-Husain and Chaudhari Chhotu Ram. The party saw the rise of the agriculture class. Majority of the Sikhs were Jats and agriculturalists. The Chief Khalsa Diwan found the racial discrimination of the Unionists against the tenets of Sikhism and refused to join the party. A few years later a section of the Sikh Jats realised that their Khatri and Arora co-religionists, being more educated got the best of the urban jobs and threw in their lot with the Unionists. Under the Unionists it was no longer good to be a Muslim, Hindu, or Sikh, or to be better qualified for a post; he had to prove that he belonged to an agricultural tribe. In the 1923 election the Akalis and Nationalists got some seats in the Punjab Legislature and Sunder Singh Majithia was re-nominated to the lieutenant governor's executive and reappointed minister of revenue. In the first elections under the new act of 1935 the Unionists again came

to power, but the Sikhs rejected both the Congress and the Unionists. Their reason was that the Congress leadership was predominantly the anti-Sikh Arya Samaj and the Unionists cardinal interest was the Muslim Jats. The Sikh leaders lacked foresight and split their votes between the Akalis and anti-Akalis (Khalsa National party). Both these parties were of no consequence.

>In 1929 the **Simon commission** visited India to review the 1919 Act and recommend new reforms. Since no Indians were associated with the commission it was boycotted and received with black flags by crowds shouting, "Simon go back." The police used force at many places to disperse mobs; at one such protest march in Lahore **Lala Lajpat Rai** (1865-1928) [born into a Hindu-Sikh family, he was the most eminent of Punjab's nationalists, an active Samajist and president of the Hindu Mahasabha for a while], was beaten and hurt badly and later succumbed to his injuries. **Bhagat Singh** later shot dead Inspector Saunders (the man allegedly believed to have assaulted the Lala). Bhagat Singh was convicted of the murder and executed on 23 March 1931. Bhagat Singh became the most famous of all terrorists in the annals of Indian revolutionary history. Mahatma Gandhi wrote, "There has never been, within living memory, so much romance round any life as had surrounded that of Bhagat Singh."

>The famous **Communal Award** (August 1932) was announced by the British Prime Minister, Mr Ramsay Macdonald. The Award introduced separate electorates, seats for various communities were fixed and the Depressed Classes (Harijans/untouchables or low-caste Hindus) were given separate representation from those of the Hindus. The Sikhs were also given weightage but not in the same measure as the Muslims; their position was as follows:

33 out of 175 in the Punjab Assembly;

03 out of 50 in the North West Frontier Province;

06 out of 250 in the Federal Legislative Assembly; and

04 out of 150 in the Council of States.

The Sikhs got nothing from the Communal Award in Sindh and the United Provinces, where they had by then sizeable populations.

>**The Poona Pact, 1932**. As the Communal Award was a great blow to the Hindu society, Mahatma Gandhi undertook a fast-onto-death. This greatly alarmed both the Hindus and the Depressed Classes. Consequently, they reached a settlement and a pact was signed at Poona between the Mahatma and Dr Ambedkar, by which they agreed to have a joint electorate. The Harijans (children of God) were given heavy weightage in mixed Hindu seats. The British Government amended the Communal Award accordingly. Gandhi called it a move to divide the Harijans from the Hindus. Dr Bhimrao Ramji Ambedkar (1891-1956) took a leading part in the framing of the Indian Constitution. Under the Constitution of India, the practice of untouchability was legally abolished. He also succeeded in obtaining special representation for the Harijans in the legislative councils of the government. Ambedkar was the first law minister of independent India in 1947, but disappointed by his lack of influence in the government he resigned in 1951. Ambedkar soon realised that the bonds between Hinduism and untouchability were very strong and deeply embedded and that Hinduism could not break the shackles of caste and untouchability. So, he toyed with the idea of converting to some other religion (including Sikhism) that did not practice untouchability.

> The immediate cause for the establishment of the **Sarab Hind Sikh Mission** in 1936 by the S. G.P.C. was the declaration made in

1935 by Dr. Ambedkar that he and his followers had decided to get out of the Hindu fold and embrace some other faith which did not practice untouchability and which would allow them a more honourable status in society. Dr. Ambedkar himself attended the first Sarab Hind Shiromani Sikh Prachar Conference at Amritsar from 11-13 April 1936. The principal objectives of the Mission were to preach the message of the Gurus among the people of all classes and castes in India and to work for the improvement of economic and social condition of converts from the so-called untouchable classes. Sikh preachers were sent out to places all over India and Missionary centres were established. Although Ambedkar and his followers ultimately decided not to adopt Sikhism, the centres, especially those at Hapur, Aligarh, Akola and Nagpur, continued to do useful work in their respective spheres. A notable accomplishment of the Mission was the establishment of the Khalsa College at Bombay in 1937. But with the passage of years the activity of the Mission dwindled. Ambedkar renounced Hinduism along with 200,000 fellow untouchables to become a Buddhist in 1951 at a ceremony in Nagpur because untouchability still continued to be a part of Hindu society.

Movements and Agitations against the British

The Congress party and Mahatma Gandhi launched a number of agitations against the British during the freedom struggle. The Sikhs, especially the Sikh element in the Congress party took part in all these movements.

Swadeshi and **Non-Co-operation Movement** by Namadhari Baba Ram Singh was the actual forerunner of these movements. The British government began to take no notice of the humble resolutions submitted by the Congress. This was followed by two calamities (the 1896 Deccan famine and the plague) and further by the Universities Act (1904) and the partition of Bengal (1905).

Against these acts of the government the Bengalis started the Swadeshi Movement. Soon the movement spread to other parts of the country and everywhere people began to discard the use of foreign goods. In its sessions of 1905 and 1906 the Congress party also adopted the Swadeshi Movement. Since then, it became the fundamental principle of the Congress to advocate the use of Swadeshi articles as far as possible and thereby harm the economic condition of England.

Satyagraha or the Non-violence Movement in 1919 was started by Mahatma Gandhi against the Rowlatt Act, but soon he was imprisoned on 06 April 1919. At many places people could not remain peaceful, so the government had to crush this movement with a heavy hand. There can be no bigger or better example of Satyagraha (non-violence) than the Sikh Gurdwara Reform Movement (1920-1925). On this issue no parallel can be drawn to the examples set by the Sikhs at Nankana Sahib, Guru Ka Bagh and Jaito. In the words of Lala Lajpat Rai, "as regards non-violence, with its attendant conception of self-sacrifice, they [Sikhs] have given the most amazing proofs at Nankana Sahib and later at Ajnala and Amritsar. They have proved themselves worthy descendants of their Gurus, and the examples they have set of self-sacrifice, calm courage, devoid of swagger, in the face of provocation, will be hard to beat."

The non-co-operation Movement (1920-21) by Mahatma Gandhi was a protest against the atrocities (Jallianwala and martial law) perpetrated by the English in Punjab. Many people in Punjab and other parts of India boycotted foreign goods and gave up their government posts, titles and everything English in character. Even students boycotted government schools and colleges.

Demand for Puran Swaraj or Complete Independence (1929) was started by the Indian National Congress after its Lahore

Session under the Presidentship of Pundit Jawharlal Nehru, wherein a resolution was passed for the complete Independence of India as against 'Dominion Status'. Accordingly, 26 January 1930 was celebrated as Independence Day all over India.

Civil Disobedience Movement (1930) commenced in February 1930 in order to achieve *Puran Swaraj* (Complete Independence) for India. Mahatma Gandhi undertook the famous **Dandi march** and violated the salt laws by preparing salt. *Hartals* (strikes) were observed and foreign goods were boycotted. The Mahatma and thousands of other people were put behind bars and the British resorted to repression. The Shromani Akali Dal on 05 March 1930 offered five thousand Akali volunteers. The campaign could not, however, be launched on account of the Hindu-Muslim riots at Calcutta and Pune. In March 1931 an understanding was reached between Gandhi and Lord Irwin. Vide the Gandhi-Irwin Pact the Civil Disobedience Movement was called off and all political prisoners set free. As no decision could be reached regarding the joint or separate electorates and the number of seats for various communities at the Second Round Table Conference the Mahatma returned from London without a settlement. He was soon arrested, and oppression restarted. This led to the restart of the Civil Disobedience Movement in 1932. In August 1932 the British Prime Minister, Mr. Ramsay Macdonald announced the **Communal Award** by which separate electorates were introduced, seats for various communities were fixed and **the Depressed Classes were given separate representation from those of the Hindus**. The **Government of India Act 1935** was passed by the British Parliament. This Act gave provincial autonomy to India and introduced various changes both in the Central and provincial Governments in India.

Quit India Movement (May 1942) was the result of Japan joining the Second World War against England and America. Soon Japan was attacking the eastern borders of India. India was then a part of the British Empire so the political leaders including Gandhi felt that as long as India remained a part of English territory the Japanese would attack India. They also perceived that all the problems of India were an outcome of British presence in India. Consequently, the Quit India movement was started and the English were asked to quit India and leave them alone. Earlier in 1939 the Congress ministries had resigned, and this made Mr Jinnah advocate 'the two-nation theory' on the instigation of the English. The most confused people were the Sikhs. They were divided. Their loyalty to the Raj had been eroded by the events of the preceding twenty years but they also had stakes in the armed forces in which a large number of Sikhs were serving, and many hoped to join.

World War II and the Sikhs

The congress protested that they had not been consulted and followed the policy of sympathy-but-no-support. The Muslim League was critical but the Unionist Muslims - who were technically members of the League – expressed their unreserved support for the British. The Communists regarded the war as imperialist.

Amongst the Sikhs the loyalist Chief Khalsa Diwan promptly declared their support for the British; the Congress Sikhs followed their party line of sympathy-but-no-support and the Communist Sikhs considered the war as imperialist and their agents busied themselves disseminating anti-war propaganda among Sikh soldiers. The Akalis who were more important than all the parties put together were the most confused. They had no love lost for the British and were equally averse to the Muslim League and the

Unionists. Their main worry was the preservation of the numerical strength of the Sikhs in the armed forces. The Akali party agreed to help the government and pressed for more Sikh recruitment. The Sikh leaders were more confused than ever when it came to discussions with their own countrymen. The Hindus supported the Congress and the Muslims the Muslim League. The Muslims wanted an independent Muslim state which would inevitably occupy much of the land in which the Sikhs lived. The Congress leaders much as they desired to have the Sikhs on their side, **were not willing to concede to them the privileges they enjoyed under British rule.** The Sikh leaders had now to choose between the Congress and the Muslim League or to discard both and independently ask for an autonomous state of their own.

There were cases of indiscipline in some Sikh units and the authorities were compelled to put a temporary ban on the recruitment of Sikhs. This was the second time that the ban was imposed; the first was during the Akali agitation for gurdwaras. Recruitment into the army was an important factor for the Sikhs because traditionally they had known no occupation but war and agriculture. And the English knew how to exploit them. However, an enquiry revealed that it was the Communist infiltration in the ranks and also a sense of uneasiness concerning the formation of a Muslim State in the Punjab. Sikh "grievances" were redressed; assurances were given to the leaders that Sikh interests would be protected. A Khalsa Defense of India League was established under the maharaja of Patiala to boost recruitment. The ban on the enlistment of Sikhs was lifted.

The Indian National Army (I.N.A.) or *Azad Hind Fauj*

Towards the end of 1941 Japanese agents established contacts with leaders of Indian communities in Thailand, China, Hong Kong, Cambodia, the Philippines, Burma (Myanmar), Malaya, and

Singapore. These countries had a large Indian population that was hostile to the British. The Japanese chose Rash Bihari Bose to win Indian collaboration. Bose had lived in Japan since 1915 and had married the daughter of the chief of the Black Dragon Society. Earlier he had been associated with the Ghadr rebellion, so he was held in high esteem by the Sikhs and his name commanded the respect of patriotic Indians. Bose also showed a marked preference for Sikhs.

Bose persuaded the Japanese Government to treat the Indian prisoners with respect and hand them over to him. Major Fujiwara of the Japanese intelligence was appointed liaison officer; his bureau came to be named after him as the Fujiwara Kikan. Bose followed in the wake of the advancing Japanese armies and established branches of the Indian Independence League. The Japanese armies repulsed the opposing British-Indian forces across the Thai-Malayan border. Captain Mohan Singh of the 1st/14th Punjab Regiment was among the thousands of captured soldiers. Captain Mohan Singh (b. 1909) was a Jat of Ghuman sub-caste of village Ugoke in Sialkot district and had joined the army in 1927 as an ordinary sepoy. He was elevated to the rank of general and given command of the I.N.A. comprising of the Indian prisoners of war. The first brigade of the I.N.A. spearheaded the Japanese attack on Singapore and seized it on 15 February 1942. Mohan Singh moved his headquarters to Singapore.

With the passage of time differences arose between Mohan Singh and the Japanese government. Mohan Singh wanted to find out the precise role the I.N.A. was to play vis-a-vis India and Japan. Colonel Iwaguro, who had succeeded Colonel Fujiwara as liaison officer, said quite bluntly that his government did not intend to make any more statements. Apart from this there were other factors like the Japanese censored I.N.A.s radio broadcasts; their treatment of Indian prisoners had become harsh; they had taken over Indian evacuee property in Burma; the Japanese commander of Singapore assumed direct control of I.N.A. personnel; and attempts were made to "nipponize" (Japanize) the 1st Division of the I.N.A. Mohan Singh's relations with the too-nipponized Rash Bihari Bose cooled. The Council of Action again submitted a memorandum to Colonel Iwaguro demanding official recognition of the Indian Independence League, the Council of Action, the I.N.A., and an unequivocal statement on Japanese policy towards India. Iwaguro lost patience. "When work is to be done, there is no time to think of legal quibbles," he retorted.

Mistrust grew on both sides. Many of Mohan Singh's colleagues particularly Colonel Narinjan Singh Gill (b. 1906, a Jat from village Majitha in Amritsar district. He was trained at Sandhurst and received the King's commission in 1925) who had been put in charge of Burma (today's Myanmar) came under suspicion. In December 1942 Gill was arrested. Mohan Singh dissolved the I.N.A. and resigned. He too was put under arrest. After two months of detention in a bungalow, the general was taken to an island where he was kept till December 1943 and then sent to Sumatra, where the British re-arrested him. He was brought to Delhi in November 1945 and released unconditionally in May 1946. In 1962 he was elected member of Rajya Sabha. Narinjan Gill was appointed Indian ambassador to Ethopia in 1955 and then to Thailand. The I.N.A. had a high proportion of Sikhs (perhaps over one-third of the total strength). With the exit of these men, Sikh enthusiasm for I.N.A. waned. Rash Bihari Bose tried to reconstitute the I.N.A.; but the spirit had withered in the men. He retired from the scene in June 1943; when Subhas Chandra Bose arrived from Germany.

Subhas Chandra Bose (1897-1945) took over the Indian Independence League and became supreme commander of the Azad Hind Fauj. At a rally in Singapore Subhas Bose announced the establishment of the Provisional Government of Azad Hind (Free India) comprising of four ministers and eight representatives of the armed forces with himself as the head of state. This Provisional Government was recognised by the Axis powers and their satellites. In the Provincial Government there were three Sikhs – two officers Nripendra Singh Bhagat and Lieutenant Colonel Gulzara Singh and one civilian, Ishar Singh Narula of Bangkok. The Japanese had learnt some lessons and mellowed down and were more co-operative with Bose's I.N.A. than they were with General Mohan Singh's and as the tide of war turned the co-operation kept increasing. Subhas Bose's popularity increased, and he began to be addressed as *Netaji* (beloved leader). The Andaman and Nicobar were transferred to the Azad Hind Government.

Bose moved his headquarters to Rangoon and in early February 1944 the I.N.A. fought the British forces on the Burma-India front and repulsed them into Indian Territory. The offensive carried on for two months with the aim of capturing Imphal; however, the arrival of the monsoons found the I.N.A. on the retreat. Subhas Bose had two more brigades trained and in January 1945 the Azad Hind Fauj fought its second round with the British 14th army on the Irrawaddy. The performance of the second Azad Hind Fauj was poorer than the first. Desertions, surrenders, deaths and disease took a heavy toll and depleted its numbers. The poor performance of the I.N.A. can be attributed to its badly fed, ill-equipped, and outnumbered force. Around mid-May 1945, the "heroic" epic of the I.N.A. came to an inglorious end. Bose retreated from Rangoon to Singapore and from Singapore to Bangkok and on 18 August

1945, the plane carrying him to Tokyo crashed in flames, thus ending his flamboyant career.

After the war a large number of soldiers and officers of the Azad Hind Fauj were imprisoned and tried by a special court. Three officers Dhillon, Sehgal and Shah Nawaz were charged for treason and tried in the historic Red Fort of Delhi. Nehru personally organised the defense and, after the officers were acquitted, arranged for them to tour the country. They were greeted by mammoth crowds wherever they went.

Cripps Mission, End of World War II and Pakistan becomes a Reality

The Japanese armies were rapidly marching across Asia, their planes were bombing Calcutta (Kolkata) and Madras (Chennai) and the I.N.A. and Japanese brigades were ready to pounce on the Indo-Burmese border. The British realised the risk to the country. Sir Stafford Cripps (a much-admired man in India) was sent to prevail upon the Indians to co-operate.

The Cripps Mission (March-April 1942) failed because it did not propose any immediate transfer of power to India. The two main proposals of the mission were that as soon as the war was over a body of elected Indians would be invited to frame a new constitution for India and if any province wished to opt out of the Indian Union it could do so. The Congress rejected it on the plea that they had no share in the control of the Defense Department, the Muslim League because Pakistan was not conceded, and the Sikhs interpreted it in a way that formation of Pakistan had been accepted. The Sikhs lost all hope and thought that their cause had been betrayed. They were ready to resist by all means the separation of Punjab from the Indian Union and pinned all their trust on the Congress party. But their faith was soon shaken when a senior and respected leader of the Congress C. Rajagopalachari got a resolution passed in the Madras Legislative Assembly that the Muslim claim for a separate state should be conceded. Rajagopalachari was forced to resign, and Gandhi launched the Quit India movement in August 1942. The Congress leaders including Gandhi were arrested and the party was declared illegal.

Rajagopalachari had driven the wedge for the division of India and it only needed hammering by the Muslim League. The viceroy now turned to other parties willing to collaborate in the war effort. The ban on the Communist party was lifted (most of the Punjabi Communists were Sikhs) and they supported the Muslim demand for Pakistan. The death of Sir Sikander Hayat Khan the leader of the Unionist party of Punjab in December 1942 removed another barrier in the way of Mr. Jinnah. In the summer of 1943, another blow was struck when the Muslim League succeeded in forming a government in the North West Frontier Province. Now it was only Sir Khizr Hayat Khan Tiwana (who succeeded Sir Sikander Hayat) of the Unionist party in the Punjab, who stuck to his guns for a united Punjab. Mr. Jinnah brought all the Muslim pressure he could to bear down on him. He visited Lahore and demanded that Khizr Hayat Khan relinquish the title "Unionist" and described his government as a "Muslim League coalition." Khizr refused. He was expelled from the Muslim League in 1944. His Muslim following began to dwindle and his ministry was reduced to a minority. His government had to rely on Congress and Akali support for survival.

Meanwhile C. Rajagopalachari drove the wedge deeper into the heart of united India on 10 July 1944 by publishing his "formula." The formula provided that if the Muslim League supported the demand for immediate independence of India, a commission would be constituted to demarcate those contiguous districts in the northwest and northeast of India where Muslims were in an absolute majority and then a plebiscite in those areas would decide whether the people wanted a separate state or not. Rajagopalachari also claimed that Mahatma Gandhi agreed with him.

Considering the position occupied by these two men in the Congress party, the Sikhs assumed that Congress had conceded Pakistan. They reacted violently. At a meeting in Amritsar on 20 August 1944 Gandhi was criticised. Master Tara Singh stated that Sikhs were a nation. A resolution demanding "a Sikh independent sovereign state" was rejected as an unviable and an "impossible demand." Sardar Ujjal Singh and Gyani Kartar Singh said explicitly that the "Azad Punjab" was only a countermeasure to the formation of Pakistan. 03 September 1944 was observed as a "protest day" and all Sikh groups were asked to form a united front.

On 07 May 1945 Nazi Germany laid down arms and on 02 September 1945 the war ended with the surrender of Japan. After the surrender of Germany, the authorities felt that the time had come to make another attempt to win over the Indian politicians. The Cripps proposals were renewed and Lord Wavell, the new viceroy invited 21 Indian leaders, including Master Tara Singh, to meet him. The leaders met at Simla in the last week of June 1945, but the conference broke down on the insistence of Jinnah that only the Muslim League should represent Indian Muslims on the Executive Council – a claim which was untenable.

Jinnah's stand at Simla and previous actions convinced Congress leaders of the futility of trying to convince or collaborate with the Muslim League. It also dawned on them that because of the persistent demand of Pakistan by the Muslims, Jinnah would have to be given the right to secede from the Indian Union provided he did not drag others who did not want to do so. If this was granted it would lead to the division of Punjab and Bengal. The Sikhs would be the biggest sufferers and the worst hit. The carving knife would fall on the Sikhs' jugular vein. Their rich agriculture land and property in West Punjab would go to Pakistan and the Sikhs would be divided leaving substantial bodies of Sikhs on both sides of the boundary. The Sikhs too, perhaps, realised that all parties were working on self-interest and they would have to extract the best bargain.

Prelude to Partition of India

In 1946 the political power in England changed from Conservative to the Labour Party and the Prime Minister Mr. Attlee was determined to give India independence. The winter elections of 1945-46 were important in the history of India. A free and united India was the salient feature of the Congress party manifesto. The Muslim League went to the polls with Pakistan as the main agenda. And the Sikhs fought the election to oppose the formation of Pakistan. The Congress registered a massive victory in the elections but failed to dislodge the Muslim League's hold on the Muslim masses. The League won every single Muslim seat in the Central Legislature and in the provinces also (except the North West Frontier Province-N.W.F.P.) 90% of the Muslim electorate was with the Muslim League. The scene that emerged was simple and clear; the non-Muslims wanted a united India and the Muslims an India divided in two nations – India and Pakistan.

In Punjab a Panthic Pratinidhi board representing all parties save the Communists was constituted to fight the election with the main purpose of opposing the formation of Pakistan. The Sikh electorate voted for the Panthic party *en masse* and the Communists (the only Sikh group supporting the creation of Pakistan) were completely trounced. The situation that evolved was that out of a total of 175 seats, the Muslim League secured 79, the Congress 51, Panthic candidates 22, Unionists and Independents 10 each (there were by-elections in the remaining 03), Sir Khizr Hayat Khan managed to re-form the government with a slender majority consisting of Unionist Muslims with Congress and Panthic support. But Sir Khizr Hayat Khan fought a losing battle against the ever-rising communal passions. On 24 January 1947, he banned private armies which included the Hindu R.S.S.S., the Sikh Akali Dals and the Muslim League National Guards. The League seized the opportunity and defied the order. He had to retrace his steps, withdraw his orders and release the leaders. It was an ignoble humiliation. He submitted the resignation of his government on 02 March 1947.

A ***Cabinet Mission*** comprising of three members of the British Cabinet, *viz.* Sir Stafford Cripps, Pethick-Lawerence and A.V. Alexander was sent to study the situation in India. Major Short, who had earned the reputation of being a friend and adviser of the Sikhs, accompanied the mission. (His famous words were 'settle the Sikhs and you settle India'). In a debate on the subject of independence of India the prime minister of England stated: "We are mindful of the rights of minorities and the minorities should be able to live free from fear. On the other hand, we cannot allow a minority to place their veto on the advance of the majority." (Mr. Jinnah's rejoinder to these words was that Muslims were not a "minority" but a "nation.")

The Cabinet Mission first interviewed Indian leaders. The Sikhs were represented by Master Tara Singh, Gyani Kartar Singh, Harnam Singh (a lawyer from Lahore), and later by Baldev Singh, then development minister in the Punjab Government. The Sikh delegation opposed the formation of Pakistan and impressed on the Cabinet Mission the utter impossibility of the Sikhs either living in a Muslim state or having territory inhabited by them handed over to the Muslims. Master Tara Singh said that he was for a united India; but if Pakistan was conceded, he was for a separate Sikh state with the right to federate with India or Pakistan. Gyani Kartar Singh elaborated the latter as a "province of their (Sikhs') own where they would be in a dominant or almost dominant position." He further gave out the geographical area of this province. Baldev Singh called the Sikh state, **Khalisthan** and spelled out its areas and boundaries. The Cabinet Mission took the Sikh demand for Sikhistan, Azad Punjab or Khalistan lightly because the way it was worded, it seemed only an argument against Pakistan and not as something seriously desirable.

As no unanimous decision could be reached the mission gave its own proposals on 16 May 1946. These proposals were based on the widest area of agreement between the parties and which, they hoped would constitute a basis on which the Indians themselves might decide the future constitution of India. Some of its main recommendations were: (i) India was to be a federation comprising both the Indian states and British India and was to deal with foreign affairs, defense and communications. (ii) A constituent Assembly to be elected by members of the provincial legislatures to draft a constitution for the country. (iii) While the constitution was being drafted an interim government consisting of all parties should look after the administration of the country.

Constituent Assembly – The elections to the Constituent Assembly were held in July 1946 as recommended by the Cabinet Mission and the Congress bagged majority of the seats. Nehru disagreed with the grouping of provinces which had been accepted by the Muslim League. Constituent Assembly was to be in three sections–(i) representatives of non-Muslim majority provinces, (ii) representatives from Punjab, the N.W.F.P. and Sindh and (iii) representatives of Bengal and Assam. He was more eager on the drafting of the constitution. Jinnah offered to form an interim government and, on the viceroy's unwillingness to invite him to do so, he rejected the May 16 proposals in toto. On 16 August 1946 the Muslim League observed the '**Direct Action Day**' in order to achieve Pakistan. Communal riots broke out in Bengal and various other parts of the country. These riots made it clearer than ever before that the partition of the country was inevitable.

Interim Government – The Congress was invited to form the government. The Congress failed to win over Jinnah but **under repeated assurances of support to minorities, particularly the Sikhs, succeeded in persuading the Sikhs to give up their opposition.** Four Sikhs had been elected to the Constituent Assembly. An interim government under Nehru was formed on 02 September 1946. Baldev Singh was the lone Sikh in the cabinet with the defense portfolio. The Muslim League now realised the hazard of allowing power to remain exclusively in the hands of the Congress and a few weeks later, when Hindu–Muslim riots flared up, the Muslim League decided to join the government. It was reconstituted on 26 October 1946. The conflict between the Congress and the Muslim League, however, continued. Lord Wavell warned the Indian leaders that civil strife had assumed such proportions that neither the police nor the army could be relied on to act impartially.

Declaration of 20th February 1947 – In view of the impasse which had been reached, Mr. Attlee announced in Parliament on 20 February 1947 that the British Government would relinquish power in India by June 1948 at the latest. While the political discussions were going on, inter-communal violence in India assumed the proportions of a civil war.

Status of the Sikhs – Sir Stafford Cripps made a lengthy statement in the British Parliament on 18 July 1946. Regarding the Sikh he said: "It was a matter of great distress to us that the Sikhs should feel they had not received the treatment which they deserved as an important section. The difficulty arises, not from anyone's underestimation of the importance of the Sikh community, but from the inescapable geographical facts of the situation. What the Sikhs demand is some special treatment analogous to that given to the Muslims. The Sikhs, however, are a much smaller community, 5,500,000 against 90,000,000, and are not geographically situated so that any area as yet desired.... can be carved out in which they would find themselves in a majority."

CHAPTER- 5

PARTITION AND INDEPENDENCE

The Sikh Dilemma

It was now evident that the partition of the country was inevitable. There were two main parties to this plan of partition - the Congress and the Muslim League – but another community much less numerous but of greater importance – the Sikhs had to be considered. All this time, the Sikhs had stood for an *Akhand Hindustan* (undivided India) and they had vehemently opposed the formation of Pakistan. The Sikhs were the most prosperous community in India; their people, land and property was distributed all over Punjab and not concentrated in any particular area of Punjab. The Sikh population was so distributed that any partition of this province would inevitably divide them into two almost equal parts. The valiant Sikhs formed about an eighth of the population of the Punjab; there were two million Sikhs in east Punjab and 1.8 million in west Punjab. The partition plan envisaged would divide the strength of the Sikhs and leave them in a minority in both the areas.

Sikhs and Punjabi Hindu members of the Central Legislature, the Punjab Assembly, and the Constituent Assembly passed a resolution demanding a "just and equitable" division of the province based on numbers and property. According to Lord Mountbatten the future of the Sikhs had been of the greatest concern to the members of the British parliament. On the question of division of Punjab on the basis of property Mountbatten said that it could hardly be expected that the Labour Government in England would subscribe to partition because of property. Any notion that the Sikh leaders might have had of pressing their case in terms of the land they owned or revenue they paid should have been dispelled by this statement. The terms of reference of the Boundary Commissions were to demarcate contiguous Muslim majority areas and in so doing consider "other factors." The Sikhs pinned their hopes on the "other factors" besides the incidence of population clause. They thought that the introduction of these two words would help them salvage their shrines, homes, lands and property in western Punjab and the boundary may run along the river Chenab. Unhappy and puzzled people clutch at straws. Their low spirits and desperation make them persist in holding on to their cherished illusions rather than looking at the pragmatic reality.

The formation of Pakistan and the division of the country entailed that either the Sikhs keep Punjab united and form a part of Pakistan or divide Punjab and become a part of India. Alternately they could also ask for a separate, autonomous Sikh state. The plight of the Sikhs aroused the sympathy of many British parliamentarians. On 15 July, R.A. Butler said in the House of Commons: "The British had the happiest possible relations with the Sikh community and, of all the martial races of the world; the Sikhs probably had built up the greatest reputation. The only situation which could mitigate the plight of the Sikhs was that the Boundary Commission should so define the boundary that the maximum portion of the Sikhs should be included within the conglomerate whole." (The Tribune, 16 July 1947).

The Sikhs saw that the partition of India meant substantially and irrevocably the partition of the Sikhs, and they felt themselves to be sacrificed on the altars of Muslim ambition and Hindu opportunism. The Sikhs also believed that they would be expropriated and massacred in West Punjab and smothered by the Hindus and Congress generally in East Punjab. They perceived that the entity of the Sikhs was being threatened on account of the persistent demand of Pakistan on the one hand and of the danger of absorption by the Hindus on the other. The Congress leaders desired to have the Sikhs on their side. Jinnah gave the Sikhs sops, but it was not the niceties of religious dogma but the call of historical memories and recent incidents (specially the opposition to Pakistan, March 1947 riots and the dispute over Shahidganj) that had to be borne in mind while taking a decision. Shaidganj was the notorious *nakhas*, the horse market of Lahore where hundreds of innocent Sikhs were publicly beheaded; later it was named Shaidganj (place of martyrdom). It was claimed by the Muslims to be a mosque and by Sikhs to be a gurdwara. Sikhs won the case and demolished remnants of the old mosque. Many a time Jinnah had made it quite clear that Pakistan was to be a purely Muslim state. The Sikhs judged that the intention of Jinnah and the Muslims was like a sportsman who is careful not to disturb the birds he means to shoot. They believed the Muslims would try to make the Sikhs of West Pakistan secure and then set about them in earnest. It was a ruse to lure and trap the Sikhs in a snare. They were afraid of becoming a helpless minority in united Punjab (Pakistan) under the Muslims who were out to destroy them. Since they felt that Pakistan meant total death for the Sikh *panth* (Sikh community), they ultimately decided that they would rather have the Punjab divided than live in Pakistan. It cannot be too often repeated that the Sikhs chose the lesser of two evils – partition or Muslim domination.

As far as a free, sovereign Sikh state was concerned, the Sikhs were not serious, and the British took it simply as a point in an argument against Pakistan. Neither did the Sikhs nor the British give it any serious thought or consideration; both took it lightly. The demand for *Khalistan* had risen off and on. In the spring of 1946, when the Cabinet Mission came to India, Master Tara Singh,

Gyani Kartar Singh and Sardar Baldev Singh raised the demand for *Khalistan* with them. In early 1947 Akalis and Communists (who supported Pakistan) put forward the claim to a Sikh state, Khalistan. An Akali circular in mid-1947 said that the Sikhs were determined on a free sovereign state with the Chenab and the Jumna as its borders (Note on Sikh Plan, p.25). These claims were however feeble and never supported or demanded forcefully by the whole Sikh *panth* (Community). Sikh leaders allowed themselves to be guided by the leaders of the Congress and did not press the case for a sovereign Sikh state with sincerity. They did not get Congress support to establish Khalistan; in fact, the Congress ensured that they did not press for it. They were indeed fooled and deceived by the Congress.

Using Khalistan as a bargaining counter could have been the best way to get concessions. Every community has a right to self-determination and a right to property. The formation of a Sikh state, even within the Union of India in those crucial years when the British were relinquishing power, would have put the Sikhs on a better footing and the map of India (as far as the states are concerned) would have been quite different. Punjab would have been a much larger state. The attention of the Sikhs was more occupied with the formation of Pakistan and the division of Punjab. When the rioting started on a large scale their focus turned to the disturbances and the disorder and lawlessness that was created. Their main concern was to avenge the excesses being committed by the Muslims. In 1947 "Mountbatten asked about Sikh motives. Was the object to set up a Sikh state? V.P. [Menon] replied no. Politically they had lost out and had not even gained the Jullundur division. Their motive was entirely revenge." (Campbell Johnson, Mission with Mountbatten, p.191). What they did not understand was that no safeguards, however strong, could be substituted for nationhood which was their birthright. They lacked forethought and did not look into the future and comprehend that this would become a crucial issue in times ahead and more and more difficult and formidable to attain.

Neither as individuals nor as a community had the Sikhs played any noteworthy part in Indian national politics before 1947. Unversed in national politics, divided in their attitude to the British – The Sikhs had neither the training nor the experience to cope with the problems of partition. The Sikh leaders lacked foresight and political acumen; they played their political cards before 15 August, very badly. So badly in fact, that there were many people in high positions who thought that they were exhausted as a major political factor and could be ignored. Even today the Central Governments of India complain of the political incompetence of the Sikhs. The Sikhs are simple people who act before they think.

The Sikhs were going to be a very small minority in the Union of India. Their leaders were divided and myopic; some of them did fear economic absorption by the Hindus; also, religious absorption. In short, the Sikhs feared (perhaps correctly) virtual extinction as a political force; and survival as a rapidly dwindling religious sect of Hinduism. A little cogitation would have told them that times change and with the change in time people change; their priorities and values change, and their promises also change. Nevertheless, the dye was cast; the Sikhs had decided to throw in their lot with India and to swim or sink with them.

Communal Riots

Riots were a common feature in India but the communal riots of 1946-47 were different in every way; they were massacres. No one was exempted on grounds of age or sex. No quarter was given to women and children and even the infants, sick, wounded and aged were not spared. Women were molested, raped, abducted and murdered. There were forcible conversions. The killings of the partition days were master-minded by politicians and executed by trained gangs armed with firearms and hand-grenades.

On "direct action day" (16 August 1946) organised by the Muslim League, riots broke out in Calcutta. Along with the Hindus some Sikhs were also killed in the first few days (Sikhs helped rescue both Hindus and Muslims and gave them shelter in their gurdwaras). Despite the Sikh loss of life and suffering, the Sikhs won the confidence of the Muslims and Hindus. Chief Minister Suhrawardy in a statement to the press praised the Sikhs for the part they played in rescuing the Muslims and exonerated them of the charge of being anti-Muslim. Even today the Sikh taxi drivers in Calcutta are a most trusted lot of people. Some of them own fleets of taxis and their drivers will invariably tell you, "*Yeh Sardarji ke taxi hai*" (This taxi belongs to a Sardarji). From Calcutta the rioting spread to other parts of India particularly Mumbai and Ahmedabad and then to east Bengal. In these places Muslims were in a majority and the victims Hindus. The news spread and in Bihar where the Hindus were in greater numbers the Muslims were killed. A pogrom was planned in Garhmukhteshwar (U.P.) and hundreds of Muslim peasants were massacred in a day.

The mutual hatred and mistrust of the Sikhs and Muslims was ages old. The Muslims quite rightly began to look upon the Sikhs as an aggressively anti-Muslim element because historical memories still persisted, they were a part of the Hindu social system, their sympathies were manifestly Hindu, and the Muslims regarded them as a militant wing of the Hindus. The Sikh attitude to Pakistan was of uncompromising hostility (the formation of Pakistan would mean devastation for the Sikhs; under no conditions could they accept Pakistan). Sikh opposition to the formation of Pakistan was constructed as animosity towards

Muslims, since the vast majority of Muslims wanted Pakistan. Muslims felt that Pakistan could bring prosperity to its people by snatching from the Sikhs, the rich agricultural lands possessed by them.

The Sikhs were practically uninvolved in the riots in Calcutta, east Bengal, Bihar, U.P., or Central India. They did not get sucked into the whirlpool of communal strife till late 1946 in Hazara (N.W.F.P.). In order to take revenge for the slaughter of their co-religionists in Bihar, the Muslims wreaked their vengeance on the innocent Sikhs (mild Khatri and Arora shopkeepers) who were a minuscule minority against the 95% Muslims. In December 1946 a large number of Sikh villages in Hazara district were destroyed. Sikh refugees began to pour into central and eastern Punjab carrying with them sordid tales of woe.

Overall, the Sikhs were the worst sufferers of the partition riots. Unsupported by friends and harassed by their enemies, they became special targets of Muslim fanatics who singled them out for fire and sword. The beginnings were in Calcutta and then came the N.W.F.P. (where Sikhs were in a helpless minority), the Muslims began in the winter of 1946-47 a regular crusade to drive or wipe them out. Their houses and property were looted and burnt, and their men, women and children were indiscriminately put to the sword or burnt alive.

Since the declaration of 20th February 1947 communal riots had become a common feature all over India. The Muslim League deliberately followed a programme of loot, murder and arson. On 02 March 1947 when Khizr Hayat Khan (the man who was against the partition of Punjab and creation of Pakistan) submitted the Unionist government's resignation, there was great excitement outside the Punjab Legislative Assembly building in Lahore. Master Tara Singh (not a member of the Assembly) unsheathed his kirpan before the crowd and shouted, "Death to Pakistan." Two days later Hindu and Sikh students clashed with a Muslim mob and later rioting started in Amritsar, Rawalpindi (the village Kahuta was completely demolished and Muslims in the area seemed pleased with themselves), Gujarat, Multan and Cambellpur. Easily identifiable Sikhs were the largest victims of the March riots. A dastardly Muslim would stealthily creep up to an unsuspecting Sikh, stab him and take to his heels. In March 1947, all limits were crossed when planned murders and arson were begun and Hindus and Sikhs were murdered in cold blood. Large parts of the cities of Amritsar and Lahore were set on fire and reduced to heaps of ruin and rubble. By summer, the whole Muslim population was up against the Sikhs in the trans-Ravi districts. This carried on till the creation of Pakistan (15 August 1947) and even afterwards, the Sikhs were killed at sight wherever found. The British Government was completely paralyzed and failed to check the disturbances or protect the Sikhs. It was thus a state of an all-out-war of extermination against the Sikhs who had been taken unawares and unprepared. The requests and pleading by Indian leaders failed to appeal to the minds of the leaders of the Muslim League. The communal bent of mind of the 74% Muslim Punjab police force was an important factor in the killings.

The March riots awakened the Sikhs from their slumber. Their armies – the Akali Dal, Akal Fauj, or Akal Sena had proved to be defunct and their leaders paper tigers. The Sikhs had been badly mauled and humiliated and had taken a terrible beating. The fear that their names had once aroused had vanished; their past glories and martial valour was taken as the rant of a decaying race. The disgrace and shame heaped upon them steeled their hearts against the Muslims; they were now bent on retaliation and settling scores. Henceforth they started preparing in real earnest and waited for the clarion call.

While the boundary commissions were holding their deliberations, the law-and-order situation in the Punjab continued to deteriorate. The militant organisations of the Hindus (R.S.S.S.), Sikhs (Akali Dal) and Muslims (National Guards-Khaksars) stepped up their preparations. On Baisakhi day (13 April 1947) Master Tara Singh and 280 *jathedars* (group/band leaders) vowed at the Akal Takht to sacrifice their lives for the *panth.* The formation of *jathas* in villages armed with the traditional *kirpan* and the spear was the real build-up of Sikh militarism. It was clear without a shadow of a doubt that as soon as the boundary line was drawn, the Muslims and Hindus would be at each other's throats and there would be an exchange of population.

On both the Indian and Pakistan sides horrible atrocities were committed. Exhausted pedestrian convoys of refugees were ambushed and attacked till the roads were jammed with the dead; trains were assaulted and sent across the borders with bogies packed with slaughtered passengers. No one was spared. Young women were occasionally let off only to be ravished later. On Independence Day (15 August 1947), the Muslim police in East Punjab was disbanded and the Muslims left to the mercy of marauding bands of Sikhs and R.S.S.S. militia. The Sikhs possess a religious solidarity unrivalled by any other community, a strong martial tradition and a discipline under leadership which renders them, even in small numbers, much more formidable than their enemies. The Sikhs are generally peace-loving people and averse to bloodshed. They abhor murder and carnage, but the Muslim League understood no language other than cold steel and this forced the Sikhs to take this unsavoury step.

On seeing their homelands partitioned the Sikhs (now prepared and aroused) were amongst the most fearless and blood thirsty participants in the massacre and migrations that ensued. They let loose a reign of terror among the Muslim population and were ruthless, brutal and merciless in slaughtering their opponents. Sikh violence attained its peak in September 1947. Mr. Jinnah (a Khoja/Bora Muslim) and the Muslim League had underestimated the Sikhs. The only language they understood was that of brutal retaliation and uncompromising hostility. Jinnah now cried to put a stop to the forces of violence that he and the Muslim League had let loose against the non-Muslims.

Never in the history of the world was there a bigger exchange of population attended with so much bloodshed. The total loss of life on both sides in the great holocaust of 1946-47 is estimated to be around 200,000 and property at about twenty thousand million rupees.

Independence

Taking various facts and factors into consideration, the Sikhs, under no circumstances could have lived with the Muslims in Pakistan. When the formation of Pakistan became inevitable, the Sikhs agreed for the partition of Punjab. There was no other way out for them. Lord Mountbatten got this confirmed himself and through various sources and after it was ascertained, he got convinced that the Sikhs in fact wanted a partition of the Punjab; he affirmed it and apprised the British prime minister and parliament. On a number of occasions in his talks and writings Lord Mountbatten while referring to the partition of Punjab added 'which the Sikhs themselves desire'; he was aware of the disastrous fate that awaited the Sikhs. The Sikhs too were not unaware of the fate awaiting them; they had no choice but to choose between Scylla and Charybdis.

Lord Mountbatten made an important declaration on 03 June 1947 regarding the partition of the country. The **Declaration of 03 June**

1947 had four main points: (i) India was to be partitioned. (ii) There would be a referendum in N.W.F.P. and in the districts of Sylhet in Assam to ascertain whether their inhabitants wanted to join India or Pakistan. (iii) The Provincial Legislature of Punjab and Bengal would decide whether these provinces were to be partitioned or not. (iv) The native states were to join either India or Pakistan as they desired.

On the basis of the declaration on 03 June 1947 the British Parliament passed the Indian Independence Act in July 1947. The chief provisions of this Act were as follows: (i) India and Pakistan were to become independent on August 15, 1947. (ii) Two dominions of India and Pakistan were to be established and their Constituent Assemblies were to decide whether to remain within the British Commonwealth of Nations or not. (iii) The Legislature of both the domains was to be fully empowered to pass any law they desired.

The claims and views of the Muslims and non-Muslims on the location of the line of partition were completely at variance with each other; Lord Mountbatten was under pressure for time and had come to India with plenipotentiary (complete) powers. He left the decision to demarcate the boundary to Sir Cyril Radcliffe (Chairman of the Boundary Commission). Radcliffe appointed boundary commissions and set about his task to define the boundary. Along with the upper reaches of the Sutlej, Beas, and Ravi, Radcliffe gave 13 districts to East Punjab (districts of Ambala and Jullundur division, Amritsar district and some tehsils of Lahore and Gurdaspur); the rest (62% of the total area of the province of Punjab and 55% of the population), he gave to Pakistan.

The Radcliffe award was as fair as it could be to the Muslims and the Hindus. The one community to which no boundary award could have done justice without doing injustice to others was the Sikhs. Their richest lands, over 150 historical shrines, and half of their population were left on the Pakistan side of the dividing line. The Sikhs had not viewed partition as being based on population alone. They banked upon property, land owned, revenue paid, military prestige, past and present services to the nation and also consideration of their status before annexation of the Punjab, their present status in the country, their influential position in the province based on historical, political, economic and various other facts. Along with this was their high education level and economic importance in central and colony districts which entitled them to a considerably greater degree of representation than was indicated by numbers alone otherwise great injustice would be done to them. In spite of all elements and circumstances being against them, the Sikhs persisted in holding on to their cherished illusions. Like the proverbial saying a drowning man will clutch at a straw, this was all wishful thinking and their dreams were badly shattered.

The decision to draw the boundary lines of Punjab was solely that of Sir Cyril Radcliffe, the chairman of the Boundary Commission. He told Mr Kuldip Nayar (14 August 1923 - 23 August 2018), the famous Indian journalist that he did not give Lahore to India because a confidante of his told him that if Lahore was given to India, then there would be no big city left in Pakistan.

On 15 August 1947 the British dominion over India came to an end and the country was partitioned into India and Pakistan. Lord Mountbatten and Mr. Mohammad Ali Jinnah became the first Governor-Generals of India and Pakistan respectively. As India celebrated its freedom on 15 August 1947, nearly ten million Punjabis were at each other's throats and the exchange of population was in full swing. The irony was that none of the persons dividing Punjab belonged to the province.

Exodus

In the winter of 1946-47 the first refugees from the N.W.F.P. started trekking to east Punjab. By August 1947 when rioting assumed the proportion of civil war this refugee movement became an exodus. A Boundary Force under Major General Rees assisted by Brigadier Digambar Singh Brar (India) and Colonel Ayub Khan (later president of Pakistan) with a force of two and a half divisions was tasked to control the movement of population along the four main routes viz. Narowal-Dera Baba Nanak, Lahore-Amritsar, Kasur-Ferozepur and Montgomery-Fazilka. A Military Evacuation Organisation (M.E.O.) was set up in early September of 1947. The M.E.O. and the Boundary Force tried to prevent collisions between the convoys, marching columns and movements of population from opposite directions. But despite their best efforts there were clashes.

Till September 1947 there were Sikh colonists in the large colonies of Lyallpur and Montgomery with no intentions of leaving their valuable and rich agriculture land which they had personally made cultivable out of the desert during the past generation. This area known as 'Bar' (tract of land) had large Sikh settlements. In order to avoid trouble in times to come the governor of Punjab (Pakistan) Sir Francis Mudie wanted them to be evicted at the earliest. He said, "I am telling everyone that I don't care how the Sikhs get across the border; the great thing is to get rid of them as soon as possible. There is still little sign of three lakh Sikhs in Lyallpur moving, but in the end, they too will have to go." The large colony of Sikhs in Montgomery moved, on orders, into the East Punjab, giving up their rich, fertile and invaluable lands which their fathers and grandfathers had helped to develop and make fecund with hard toil and sweat over a period of time. Most of these Sikhs had an army connection which served them well during the exodus. Their migration was an organised movement, carried out with military precautions, tactical and administrative, and it moved in good order with few casualties.

It is estimated that about 14 million Hindus, Muslims and Sikhs were displaced during the partition in the Punjab province. There was massive loss of life due to the retributive genocide. It was the largest mass migration in human history. Never in the history of the world was there a bigger exchange of population attended with so much bloodshed.

Refugee Rehabilitation

Camps were set up for refugees by the Indian Government. The biggest camp was at Kurukshetra. By October 1947 there were well over 720,000 refugees in the Indian camps. Maharaja Yadavindra Singh of Patiala offered his entire resources for the relief of the displaced people of Punjab. The resettlement of the refugees was an arduous task. A Resettlement Department staffed with about 8,000 *patwaris* (revenue officials) and rural officers was set up. Two young Sikh civilian officers Tarlok Singh and M S Randhawa were entrusted with the task of resettlement of refugees. They did a commendable job.

The government took over the vacated houses, lands and properties of the Muslim. The refugees, crossing over from Pakistan and those in refugee camps were guided to various towns and villages in order to take over the assets left behind by the Muslims. Each family irrespective of their possessions in Pakistan was granted ten acres of land and a loan to buy various agricultural needs. Initially the new governments were not sure of the exact nature of the problem i.e., whether the migration was permanent, or would the refugees return to their ancestral homes. However, with the harvesting of the Kharif crop it became amply clear that the transfer of population was in fact permanent. The temporary allotments had to be made permanent and the displaced persons compensated out of what the Muslims had left behind. Tarlok Singh produced an elaborate plan for permanent resettlement and drew up a Land Resettlement Manual. No words of praise are enough for him for the accomplishment of this herculean task.

This was no easy task as not only was the number or Hindus and Sikhs who had come out of West Punjab and the N.W.F.P. somewhat larger than the number of Muslims who had left East Punjab (4,351,477 against 4,286,755), but there was also a considerable difference, both quantitative and qualitative, in the land left behind by the Muslims; the Hindus and Sikhs had left behind 67 lac acres of the very best agricultural land; the Muslims of East Punjab left behind only 47 lac acres of comparatively poor soil. Added to the complications was the fact that in districts such as Karnal, Muslim owned land was in the possession of Hindu tenants, who were naturally reluctant to let refugees take over cultivation. In terms of the assessment of land as drawn up by Tarlok Singh the Hindu-Sikh refugee farmers who had left behind 4,000,000 units had to be compensated with less than 2,500,000 units. For a fair and equitable division of land worked out by a system of grading the small landholder incurred very little loss but the rich zamindar was reduced to modest proportions.

The division of Punjab brought about a radical upheaval in the social, economic and political fabric of the Sikh people of both the agriculture and the trading classes. From being the most prosperous community, they were reduced to the level of other Indian societies. Sikh farmers owning large estates in Pakistan's Punjab were reduced through the process of displacement; those in Indian Punjab were leveled by the process of legislation which fixed the land ceiling at a maximum of 30 acres. The trading Sikhs dwelling in urban areas were worse hit than the peasants. The property left behind by Muslims was very little as compared to what the Sikhs had left behind in Pakistan. In addition, the Sikh merchant had to compete both with the Hindu refugee counterpart and the established Hindu trader.

The Bright Side of Partition

The Sikhs were the worst sufferers of the partition. The loss of Sikh life and property was unimaginable. But every cloud has its silver lining and after rain the sun shines. Adversity had its positive redeeming features also, as follows:

- The Sikhs were the staunchest advocates of an undivided India. The Sikh leader Master Tara Singh did not play into the hands of Mr Jinnah and East Punjab was saved to become a part of India. Had it been otherwise the Land of the Five Rivers would have been completely lost to India and the fate of Jammu and Kashmir too might have been different.

- The class barriers were lowered. By giving the same amount of land to all agriculturalists, the menial classes were elevated to the level of rich Jat and Rajput farmers. The cooperative farming because of the 30-acre ceiling imposed by legislature in east Punjab carried the leveling process further. This was in consonance with the teachings of Sikhism which is an egalitarian, democratic and secular religion. It recognizes no distinction between man and man and does not believe in the caste system and advocates a society free of all caste and creed distinctions.

- Reduction in land holdings forced the owners to cultivate the land themselves. This brought in cooperative farming with modern techniques and improved seeds and fertilizer began to be used. More attention was paid to silviculture and animal husbandry. Sikh farmers took the lead and dairy and poultry farming along with the cultivation of fast-growing trees became lucrative side-line sources of income. Soon east Punjab changed from a deficit to a surplus region.

- The paucity of land and search of better avenues for trade and business made the Sikhs go to other parts of India and foreign countries. The Sikh peasants settled in the malarial jungles of Terai in Uttar Pradesh, the weed-infested regions of Madhya Pradesh, the deserts of Rajasthan and in smaller numbers in other parts of India right down to the Andaman and Nicobar Islands. Sikh refugee farmers displayed the adaptability and vigour of their colonizing forefathers in clearing the jungles and bringing barren lands under cultivation. The trading classes many of whom had been reduced to abject poverty showed the same grit and determination as the Sikh farmers in resettling themselves in their professions. They did all kinds of odd and menial jobs but begging in the streets was below their dignity. Thus, they spread all over northern India and there was hardly a place without a colony of Sikhs. And once again the Sikhs earned the respect of their countrymen as a community with fortitude and determination.

Although the Sikh migrants spread all over India and many thousands went abroad; this move from west to east Punjab helped the Sikhs to concentrate, in their original homeland where they would be more powerful than ever. This was the most significant effect of the migration.

CHAPTER- 6

AFTER INDEPENDENCE

Contribution of Maharaja Patiala in Solving Conundrums after Partition

Maharaja Yadavindra Singh of Patiala contributed significantly in solving the refugee resettlement and various other problems that followed independence. Some of his contributions are as follows:

- He offered his entire resources for the relief and rehabilitation of the uprooted people of Punjab. The organisation set up by the Maharaja assisted the government in providing relief and was of great help to the displaced Punjabis.

- In May-June 1947 India was faced with the danger of further vivisection by a proposal for the creation of another separate and independent federation of Rajasthan comprising of some Indian states. Had the youthful Maharaja of Patiala Yadavindra Singh (the pro-chancellor of the Chamber of Princes and a leading figure in the politics of Indian princes) not brought around the princes and saved the situation even Sardar Vallabhbhai Patel, the iron man of India would have found it very difficult to control.

- When the tribals from the north-west aided by regular Pakistani troops attacked the Kashmir valley in October-November 1948; the Patiala troops were flown in to defend the state soon after Maharaja Hari Singh the Dogra ruler signed the Instrument of Accession on 26 October 1947. These brave Sikhs were able to check the advance of the Pakistanis before other Indian troops arrived. This service rendered to India by the Patiala troops will remain writ large on the pages of history.

- Maharaja Yadavindra Singh of Patiala took the lead in persuading the princes to join the Indian Union. He was the right-hand man of Sardar Patel in the integration of princely states into the Union of India and in the words of Sardar Patel himself (15 July 1948), "He took up the cause of the country at a time when there were few friends amongst the princely order and he made a notable contribution to the unity and integrity of India."

Patiala and East Punjab States Union (PEPSU)

In 1948, Sikh princely states of Punjab along with Malerkotla and Nalagarh were merged into one unit to form PEPSU with the handsome Sikh Maharaja Yadavendra Singh as rajpramukh (governor) and a Sikh aristocrat Gyan Singh Rarewal as chief minister. The states that formed PEPSU were Patiala, Nabha, Kapurthla, Faridkot, Jind, Malerkotla, Nalagarh, Kalsia and areas of Kasauli, Kandaghat, Dharampur and Chail.

The two political parties - Congress and the Akalis were evenly matched in the state of PEPSU. After Gyan Singh Rarewal the congressman Raghbir Singh became the chief minister and he was followed by Brish Bhan. PEPSU had a short and unsteady life span. In PEPSU the Sikhs formed most of the population. This was a big boon for the Sikhs and their dream of forming a Sikh state; all that was required was to merge the Sikh majority areas with PEPSU and the much-desired Sikh state (*suba*) would have become a reality. But this lucrative and fortunate blessing was squandered away by the Sikh leaders when they showed deplorable lack of forethought and unity; if there was a sane voice it was suppressed. Misguided and misled, the gullible Akalis supported by the concentration of Sikh population asked for the abrogation of PEPSU. The already willing Indian government happily abolished PEPSU in 1956 and merged it with East Punjab.

Unification - The Sikh State (Punjabi Suba)

A sovereign Sikh state had never been far from the hearts and minds of the Sikh people. Since the times of Guru Gobind Singh, every day in their prayers they sang the litany *raj karega Khalsa* (The Sikhs shall rule). During the worst times of persecution in the eighteenth century; in the forests and deserts, this prayer kept their morale high. Thousands of Sikhs lost their lives to achieve this aim; exactly a hundred years after Guru Gobind Singh's call to arms in 1699 when the Sikh Kingdom was founded by Maharaja Ranjit Singh in 1799, it confirmed their belief that the Sikhs were destined to rule Punjab.

When the British were to leave India, the Sikhs believed that Punjab should be rightfully restored to the Sikhs from whom it was treacherously seized. But the English introduced the principle of rule of the majority and nothing else worked; everything was based on population alone i.e., numbers and simple counting of heads, it was the democratic will of the people and everywhere the Sikhs were in a minority. If this were to be the case, then most of India would be ruled by the Hindus and the Muslim dominated areas including Punjab by the Muslims. The Sikhs aligned themselves with the Hindus and for twenty years all their energies were spent on frustrating Muslim designs of ruling Punjab. When nothing worked, they decided to keep the Muslims at bay by agreeing to the partition of Punjab and the formation of Pakistan.

The resurgence for a Sikh state grew as the demand for Pakistan became stronger. During these crucial years when the British were taking measures to quit India the Sikh leaders allowed themselves to be guided by the leaders of the Congress and instead of boldly and sincerely demanding a sovereign Sikh state (which the Sikh masses wanted), put the claim forward only as an argument against Pakistan. The demand was feeble, and no one took them seriously. The Congress ensured that they did not press for it and thus they were fooled and deceived by the Congress. The Sikhs were one track minded and all their energies were wasted against the formation of Pakistan and later on inflating the size of the non-Muslim part of Punjab for which they advanced all kinds of arguments - historic, economic, hydrographic and geographic.

Immediately after independence of India, the Sikhs were unashamedly betrayed by the Indian National Congress. They were deceived and denied the promised "Semi-autonomous Unit" in Punjab. The Sikhs felt deep discontentment for a government that they did not trust; and resentment for the Hindus, whose suffering they minimised. The conditions that prevailed in the post-partition days forced many Sikhs to doubt the wisdom of their leaders in having joined India and thrown their lot with the Hindus and questioned, "The Muslims got Pakistan, the Hindus got Hindustan; but what did we Sikhs get?" However, the chief cause of Sikh insecurity in free India was the resurgence of Hinduism and increase in apostasy (this in fact meant regressing into Hinduism). The Indian state was in name secular but Hindu in reality. The only way the Sikhs could retain their distinct and separate identity was to have a separate state where they were in a majority. Then they could enforce the teaching of the Punjabi language, Sikh scriptures and history which would influence the minds of the younger generation and make them feel proud and cherish their Khalsa traditions. Valuable time had been lost; had they been serious they could have easily got a state (adequate in size) from the British.

After partition a situation was created in which the Sikhs became a majority in certain tehsils of east Punjab. The creation of PEPSU (where the Sikhs were in a majority) and the declaring of Punjab to be a bi-lingual state (with both Punjabi and Hindi as its languages) by the government prepared the grounds and gave an opportunity for the first time to put forward the argument of numbers in support of a Sikh state. All that was required was to add the Sikh majority areas to PEPSU and subtract the Hindi speaking areas of Haryana (which was attached to Punjab after the mutiny of 1857 and was a sandy unproductive area). It did not take the shrewd government long to realise that PEPSU had in fact become the focus of a Sikh state and that it should be liquidated and merged with Punjab. The Akali leaders were hoodwinked and believed that the merger would bring them closer to the formation of Punjabi Suba; the Sikhs praised and joined the Congress party in strength. But in a few months when reality dawned on them, they realised that this foolish step had taken them even further away from attaining their cherished goal. They now existed in a state where their strength was only 35 percent against a Hindu permanent majority of 65 percent.

The Indian National Congress had committed itself repeatedly to the principle of linguistic provinces. But after independence, its attitude to the subject changed – inasmuch as it concerned Punjab and the Sikhs. Andhra Pradesh had been created based on language and the demand for a Marathi speaking state encouraged the Sikhs to demand a Punjabi (Punjabi in Gurmukhi script) speaking state. The main demand in fact was for a Sikh state; language was only a sidetrack. Hindu organisations, especially those connected to the Arya Samaj and its political counterpart, the Jan Sang, started a movement to persuade Punjabi speaking Hindus (who knew no other language but for Punjabi) to disown their mother tongue and adopt Hindi instead – by denying their mother-tongue they set a precedence in doing something which no other people on the surface of the earth had ever done in the entire history of mankind.

At this critical juncture, Sikh leaders displayed pathetic lack of unity. All of them worked for self-interest. Master Tara Singh stood alone in his demand for a Punjabi Suba. Despite the betrayal of communal interests by many leaders, the Sikh masses stood with Master Tara Singh and gave him their support. The Congress was also fortunate in finding in the chief minister of Punjab, Partap Singh Kairon, a forceful man who was passionately opposed to the Akalis. Even though he was alone, Master Tara Singh carried on his struggle relentlessly with the support of the vast majority of Sikhs.

In May 1960 when Master Tara Singh was arrested on the orders of Kairon, he appointed Sant Fateh Singh (a *Granthi*-cum-social worker) to carry on the agitation for a Sikh state. The *sant* (saint) organised passive resistance on a massive scale and matters came to a head when he went on a fast on to death. The fast and the agitation were called off (09 January 1961) when the government promised to look into the grievances of the Sikhs. The negotiations with the government came to naught and Nehru refused to concede the demand of the Sikhs. This forced Master Tara Singh to undertake a fast unto death (15 August 1961). The government refused to yield and after 43 days, the old warrior's spirit was broken, and he gave up the fast. The Master saved his life but killed his political career and dealt a grievous blow to the cause of Punjabi Suba. The Sikhs found him guilty of proving false to his oath as well as the hallowed Sikh tradition of martyrdom and never forgave him.

Because of the Chinese aggression in 1962, the Sikhs temporarily suspended the agitation and eagerly joined in the war effort. After the war, the Sikhs found themselves still grappling with the problem of Punjabi Suba. The agitation was resumed. Sant Fateh Singh went on a fast again in December 1964. The persistence of the Sikhs and once again their contribution in men and material to the Indo-Pak war of 1965 made the government yield to their demand. The Sikh state of Punjab became a reality on 01 November 1966 on a linguistic basis.

The commission for the demarcation of boundaries (appointed in April 1966) whose decisions based on the impugned and tainted 1961 census (or was it deliberate?) gave some Punjabi speaking areas and Chandigarh (built on Sikh lands) to Haryana. Thus, there ensued another agitation for the restoration of Punjabi speaking areas and Chandigarh. Chandigarh became a union territory and capital of both states on 09 June 1968. **Sardar Darshan Singh Pheruman** courted martyrdom on the 74th day of his fasting unto death (27 October 1969). On 26 January 1970, Sant Fateh Singh the President of S.G.P.C. went on fast and threatened immolation. On February 1970, the government announced its decision to make over Chandigarh to Punjab, with certain areas of the Fazilka and Abohar tehsils of Punjab to Haryana in lieu thereof. As this was not acceptable to Punjab, the decision could not be implemented. So, the struggle is still on. After the formation of the Sikh state of Punjab, the Akalis started winning elections and forming governments in Punjab.

Punjab Rebellion or Sikh Insurgency

The insurgency in Punjab started in the late 1970s and lasted through the 1990s. The roots of the insurgency were very complex. The main factors were inadequate recognition of Sikhism and the Punjabi language and maltreatment by the Congress government ever since the inception of Indian Punjab in 1947. All schools in Punjab were teaching Punjabi children Hindi even after the linguistic reorganisation of Punjab which started creating concern among the parents and community leaders. During the Punjabi Suba movement, the Sikhs faced humiliation and difficulties. Punjabi was finally recognised as the official language of Punjab in 1966 with the creation of Punjabi Suba and the states of Himachal Pradesh and Haryana created out of it; Chandigarh (later on 09 June 1968 Chandigarh became a union territory and capital of both states) and certain Punjabi speaking areas were given to Haryana.

The Sikhs felt alienated within India and put forward a resolution known as the **Anandpur Sahib Resolution** to address all grievances they had within the Indian state. In the resolution were included both religious and political issues; the Sikhs felt that the Anandpur Resolution represented a real solution to the genuine demands of Punjab such as a larger share of water for irrigation and the return of Chandigarh (built on Sikh lands) and Punjabi speaking areas to Punjab; the resolution was rejected by the government. Sant Jarnail Singh Bhindranwale launched a *Dharam Yudh Morcha* (a peaceful march in order to implement the Anandpur Resolution) in 1982 and thousands of people joined the movement. The Congress government suppressed the mass movement with a heavy hand; over a hundred Sikhs were killed in police firings and over 30,000 arrested by security forces in two and a half months. After this, Bhindranwale decided that it was time for a militant approach to solve the problems of the Sikhs as nothing could be achieved by peaceful means and this led to the beginning of the insurgency. The main roots of the insurgency were as follows:

- The Punjabi Suba movement was the prelude to the revolt by the Sikh people. The nationwide movement of linguistic groups seeking statehood resulted in a massive reorganisation of states according to linguistic boundaries in 1956. At that time, Indian Punjab had its capital in Simla, and though most of the Sikhs lived in Punjab, they still did not form a majority. But if Haryana and Himachal were separated, Sikhs would have a Punjab in which they would form a majority of 60 per cent against the 40 per cent Hindus. The Akali Dal, a Sikh dominated political party active mainly in Punjab, sought to create a Punjabi Suba. This case was presented to the States Reorganisation Commission established in 1953.

- The Green Revolution in Punjab had several positive impacts, but at the same time the introduction of mechanized farming led to unemployment. The unemployed youth could have been absorbed by industries, but Punjab being a border state, the Indian government was reluctant to set up heavy industries there. The unemployed rural Sikh youth were drawn to the militant groups and formed the backbone of militancy.

- The then Prime Minister of India, Mrs. Indira Gandhi on the advice of Giani Zail Singh (the President of India) and Sardar Buta Singh (the Home Minister of India) used Sant Jarnail Singh Bhindranwale to their advantage to undermine the Akali Dal. The strategy backfired when 13 Sikhs in Amritsar were killed in a Nirankari - Sikh clash. Bhindranwale and his followers became a source of disruption and mayhem, but **a secret third agency was also working to make the Punjab situation unstable at the behest of the Indian Government**. Bhindranwale gained a lot of support from the Sikhs, especially rural Sikh youth, who felt alienated by the Indian government. The law-and-order situation became so bad in 1984 that Indira Gandhi had to take the help of the Indian army. This led to the infamous **Operation Blue Star**.

- Pakistan was deeply involved in training, guiding and arming of Sikh militants. The leaders of various radical groups were based in Pakistan from where they coordinated various militant activities of their outfits in Punjab and elsewhere in India under the guidance of Pak ISI. The ISI provided safe havens for shelter and dumping of weapons and explosives for the extremists.

- The disgraceful and ill-timed Operation Blue Star and its atrocities even against innocent civilians including ladies and children led to further violence and the insurgency got worse. A section of Sikhs turned to militancy in Punjab; some Sikh militant groups demanded a separate "Sikh homeland" called Khalistan; others demanded an autonomous state within India, based on the Anandpur Sahib Resolution and there were a large number of Sikhs who condemned the actions of the militants. By 1985, the situation in Punjab had become highly volatile. The Congress (I)-led Central Government dismissed its own Congress government in Punjab; declared a state of emergency, and imposed President's Rule in the state.

Operation Blue Star (03-08 June 1984)

More than 200 years after the Afghan King Abdali's destruction of the Golden Temple, in June 1984, Indian Prime Minister Indira Gandhi ordered an attack code named **Operation Blue Star (03-08 June 1984)** on armed Sikh militants holed up in the Golden Temple, the holy shrine of India's Sikh minority. The situation was intentionally brought to such a pass so that the country and the world did not doubt the motive of the attack. The attack was wrongly timed and conceived (by design or default) because the day fixed for the assault was Guru Arjan's martyrdom day and pilgrims had gathered in large numbers for the religious ceremonies. Thousands of these innocent devotees were trapped inside Golden Temple. A judicious thought had not been given to the fate of these 150,000-200,000 innocent pilgrims before launching the attack. No one till date has replied as to why such a wrong timing was chosen. On 03 June curfew was imposed in Amritsar and Punjab was cut off from the rest of India. What followed was a six-day-long armed battle between the army and the militant Sikhs. There was no plan to use tanks but when the army faced very tough opposition it was decided to launch an attack with armoured vehicles and tanks. A large number of people were killed in the ensuing firefight, which included several hundred innocent Sikh pilgrims. **It was the third *Ghallughara* (holocaust or carnage) of Sikhs, worse than the first two.**

Reports of Indian Army Soldiers tying up civilians with their turbans and shooting them in their backs were not uncommon. Brigadier Onkar Singh Goraya (retd.) in his book *'Operation Bluestar and After: An Eyewitness Account'* brings out two pertinent points regarding the dead – **one** that Sikh youth were killed by the army simply on suspicion of being terrorists and further says that this type of madness does overtake some soldiers during heat of the battle and **two** he says that he saw more dead bodies in the Golden Temple Complex on 06th June than those seen during 32 days of fighting 1965 and 1971 Wars with Pakistan. The number of terrorists in the temple was exaggerated and the number of weapons inflated. On 6 June 1984, Bhindranwale was shot dead. It must not be forgotten that Bhindranwale was initially fostered by Congress leaders for their political gain. But in spite of the reign of terror let loose in Punjab by Bhindranwale and the blunders and follies committed by him; as a person he was a man with a spotless image, devoid of corruption and free of hunger for worldly possessions, unlike many other religious and political leaders in Punjab. The state and Central government are also no less to blame for the Punjab crisis.

Sikh Insurrection

Bluestar unleashed a cycle of revenge not seen since the Partition and resulted in widespread mutiny in the Army's Sikh units. Since Bluestar and its aftermath occurred before the age of live TV in India, there is little visual evidence left but the sounds on audiotapes give you an echo of the terrible night that changed the history of India. **A lot of the evidence that did exist was destroyed by the government in power**. Sikhs around the world were outraged at the desecration of their holiest shrine. The Sikh community refused to allow the central government to repair the damage to the temple, instead undertaking the work themselves. Although the damage has been repaired, the incident has not been forgotten; the wounds of Operation Bluestar will never heal.

On the morning of 31 October 1984, four months after Operation Bluestar Prime Minister Indira Gandhi was assassinated. These two events played a major role in the Sikh and anti-Sikh violence that consumed Punjab till the early 1990s. **Indra Gandhi's assassination** was followed by the **anti-Sikh pogrom of 1984**. Angry mobs of Congress party workers and anti-national elements instigated by leaders from Indira Gandhi's Congress party attacked Sikhs in New Delhi. The orders came from the PMO (Prime Minister's Office), the aim was a Sikh carnage and extermination and poor/poverty-stricken Sikhs faced the brunt of these murderers, aided by the police and congress ministers and leaders. The mobs burned down shops and killed men indiscriminately. They raped women and wiped-out entire families. The police sided with the attackers and later seemed to have gone underground. The government seemed to have perished with its leader. It was a holocaust and 3,000 Sikhs (the official death toll) were systematically massacred after Indra Gandhi's assassination in a one-sided premediated, cold-blooded massacre. Unofficial estimates put that number at more than 7,000. The terrible aftermath of Operation Bluestar brought about political upheaval, and communal violence. The Sikhs had become refugees in their own country and felt like Jews in Nazi Germany.

The Sikhs were persecuted and the amount of damage caused to the Sikh religion was immense. It was an attack on Sikh spirit and sought to instill fear in the hearts of Sikhs with the intention of coercing them into accepting the rule of the Indian government and forsaking their freedom. It was a well-planned pogrom. No wonder, more than thirty years later, not even one of the accused was convicted for those bloody anti-Sikh riots. This holocaust of 1984 is bound to reverberate through Sikh history for a very long time to come, perhaps forever. It changed the Sikh psyche forever. Today the nation pretends as if the Sikh pogrom of November 1984 never happened.

But there was a resurgence of militancy in Punjab. Terrorism returned to Punjab and survived for a whole decade. Instead of fighting the militants, the state was fighting its own faultless people. A lot of Sikhs had to take asylum in foreign countries. In spite of being a signatory of the Geneva Convention, human-rights abuses and violations were committed by the state; heinous and brutal crimes were perpetrated against poor harmless citizens in which thousands of innocent people irrespective of age and sex perished in fake encounters while others have been languishing in jails without trial for years with unprecedented records of torture and barbarity. Neither has the number or the names of casualties ever been made public nor any compensation paid to the families of the victims. K.P.S. Gill, as director general of police in Punjab, was cited by human rights organisations as personally responsible for the widespread atrocities of torture, rape, and "encounter" killings, but remained in his post for years (*Fighting for Faith and Religion* by Cynthia Keppley Mahmood Page 208).

It is estimated that more than 12,000 people died during insurgency in Punjab. A close scrutiny will reveal that the government made use of Sikhs in a very subtle way to fight the insurgency in Punjab. These Sikhs were the two politicians Giani Zail Singh and Sardar Buta Singh, the two generals Dyal and Brar, the chief minister of Punjab Beant Singh and director general of police in Punjab K.P.S. Gill and the Punjab police. It was Sikh versus Sikh to kill and get killed while the country watched the fun. And it was the Sikh Prime Minister Manmohan Singh who was made to apologise for Bluestar and the anti-Sikh riots.

Today, Punjab is no longer India's most prosperous state that it once was. What goes up must come down. The state is fighting for its full and fair shares of river waters. There was reduction in the strength of Sikhs in the armed forces from 33 to 12 percent in 1974 on the basis of fixed quota for states. The Sikh farmers are being ousted from lands that they purchased, tamed and brought under the plough in Terrai, Rann of Kutch and elsewhere in the country; they are fighting for their rights. Many Sikhs are immigrating to foreign lands in search of better opportunities. At large the people in Punjab are seething under the menace of drugs, unemployment, farmer suicides and rampant corruption in all spheres. There are large scale conversions to Christianity among the marginalized Sikhs, the management and functioning of Gurdwaras is degenerating leaving a wide gap between concept and practice, Sikhs have forgotten the teachings of their gurus and are patronising and seeking solace in *deras* (abode or habitation) of self- styled gods and drifting away from gurdwara.

After Maharaja Ranjit Singh the Sikhs have failed to produce a dynamic leader, worth his salt. The governments in Punjab have been shamelessly corrupt and only interested in making money at any cost. Along with the police, administration, state agencies, and *goonda* (hoodlum) element they are getting youth addicted to drugs, farmers are on the roads and committing suicide. There is influx of Bihar and UP labour; exodus of Sikh youth from Punjab to foreign lands, because successive governments have left nothing for them. There is flourishing propagation and spread of Christianity. The flood of conversions to Christianity is proceeding at an alarming rate. Crime and corruption are rampant and land, sand, transport, liquor and drug mafia rule Punjab. Politics, business and crime go hand in hand. The exchequer has been drained and the tax payers/people's money is being misused for personal gain and enjoyment on frivolous pretexts and issues. The situation is pathetic.

However, the Sikh spirit of 'never say die' and to fight back still persists and they will bounce back as they have always done. The Sikhs are at their best in an adversity or crisis. The people of Punjab are no longer relying on the government and pinning their hopes on self-help and self-reliance. A lot of money is flowing in from foreign countries and many organisations are coming forward to help the people in all spheres. These organisations are doing tremendous work in the fields of education, creating job avenues/opportunities, upliftment of the downtrodden, drug de-addiction, helping farmers and in many other fields.

The Sikhs require careful handling and statesmanship that looks far into the distant future so that the same mistakes are not repeated. They feel alienated, let down and fear a threat to their distinct and separate identity and of being absorbed into the Hindu fold. They are a small minority and should be treated as a special case requiring special sympathy and special practical aid for their qualities in war and peace that have brought them renown. This cannot be recommended more forcefully than in the present times because suppression through force has never worked.

PART TWO

NOTES

1

MAHARAJA RANJIT SINGH – THE MAN AND HIS CHARACTER

Maharaja Ranjit Singh is the most popular hero of the Sikhs. He is to the Sikhs what Shivaji is to the Marathas, Napoleon to the French, Washington to the Americans and Cromwell to the British. He united a warring people, inspired them to great heights and made them masters of the land. The mighty Maharaja Ranjit Singh – the one-eyed lion of the Punjab (*Sher-e-Punjab*) came of a line of men who were warriors and was successful in every campaign he undertook. He was a great warrior and an enlightened ruler of his time. Ranjit Singh was an individual with modern vision and leadership. He was a dynamic leader and evoked intense loyalty among his subjects and his army consisting of Sikhs, Rajputs, Hindus and Muslims. He never admitted the possibility of failure, and hence held the "awe factor". His subjects loved him and were loyal to him till the last breath of his life.

Maharaja Ranjit Singh was a glittering, exotic ruler and a remarkable and extraordinary man with a charismatic personality. In a turbulent and violent age, full of tyranny, fanaticism, corruption and persecution, he was strong, tolerant, and enlightened. Ranjit Singh was one of the best monarchs with a large heart of gold; he was remarkably humane, liberal and benevolent; he was able, magnanimous, brave and ambitious and to every man he was generous and affable. He was simple in his habits, courteous in speech and utterly humble in his dealings. He respected religious men. Even at the height of his power, he did not lose the common touch.

As far as looks are concerned, he was small, dark and ugly. He had but one eye (the left eye, being lost to smallpox, which struck him at an early age), his face was pitted with smallpox and his stature certainly did not exceed 5 ft. 4 in. Emily Eden (sister of the Governor-General Lord Auckland) described Ranjit Singh as being 'exactly like an old mouse, with grey whiskers and one eye'. It is said that once his Muslim wife Moran while commenting on his ugly looks asked, "Where was your Highness when God was dispensing good looks?" "I had gone out in search of a kingdom," replied the king. His looks contributed little to his popularity. If nature had been unkind to Ranjit Singh, in endowing the gift of beauty, she compensated him in many other ways.

Although unattractive himself, Ranjit Singh was a lover of beautiful things. He surrounded himself with handsome men and beautiful women. He maintained a bevy of beautiful Kashmiri nautch girls. Actually, it was a cultural troupe (Amazon contingent) consisting of a bevy of good-looking teenage girls to amuse the Maharaja and his guests. They wore military uniforms and dressed as soldiers rode out with him on ceremonial occasions; they were also asked to stage mock combats for the Maharaja's pleasure. While visiting the Maharaja's court W. G. Osborne the military secretary to Lord Auckland; the Governor General of India (1836-42) is known to have remarked, 'Though far removed from being handsome himself, Ranjit appears to take a pride in being surrounded by good looking people, and I believe few, if any other, courts either in Europe or the East could shew such a fine-looking set of men as the principal Sikh Sardars.'

Ranjit Singh's love of the arts was equally well marked. Fakir Nuruddin (younger brother of Fakir Azizuddin) was responsible for commissioning arts all over India. As a result, the period of Sikh rule witnessed a flourishing of art. He employed artists in his court and during his campaigns gave orders to his generals to take every care to spare libraries and other places of art. This was the golden era of Sikh history. It was a period of glory and splendour.

Though small of stature and slight of built, Ranjit Singh was wiry, as if made of whipcord and full of daring. He was a man of courage and shared all dangers and fatigues with his troops; many a time, he led his men into battle and fought sword in hand, facing danger and risking his life. He admired bravery above all manly virtues and exalted the valiant. Ranjit Singh's strength did not lie in his allies, but in the strong right arm of the Khalsa. According to Burnes, Ranjit Singh said that – 'he owed all his success to the bravery of his nation, who were very free from prejudice, would carry eight days' provisions on their backs, dig a well if water were scarce, and build a fort if circumstances required it'. Horses were the ruling passion of his life; he was a superb horseman and often spent most of his day in the saddle. In fact, he spent most of his years in the saddle of a horse. He created an empire and triumphed in every campaign that he undertook. He succeeded in all his enterprises.

All his life Ranjit Singh displayed the magnanimity and generosity for which he was so well known, and which so much contributed to his success as a leader of men. He not only spared and forgave his fallen adversaries again and again, but warmly embraced them and made generous grants for their lifetime. This magnanimity always gained him well-deserved returns and, also contributed to his success as a leader of men. Thus, did he turn bitter enemies into grateful friends.

Sher-e-Punjab, Maharaja Ranjit Singh did not receive any formal education and remained unlettered to the last and like Akbar the

Great, he was completely illiterate. Though illiterate, he was extremely brave and very inquisitive. He respected men of learning and like the illiterate Akbar, made up the deficiency by seeking the company of men of letters and scholars and satisfied his craving for knowledge by badgering them with questions. He esteemed learning and learned men. Wisdom, forbearance, and broadmindedness has nothing to do with being lettered or unlettered. Alexander Burnes wrote, 'Without education and without a guide, he conducts all the affairs of the kingdom with surpassing energy and vigour, and yet he wields his power with a consideration quite unprecedented in an Eastern prince'. Though untutored, Ranjit Singh was a man of exceptional qualities; the sterling attributes of head and heart distinguished him from other men; these remarkable traits were God-gifted qualities that were inherent in him and had been gained through experience and circumstances. Enlightenment and tolerance, it would seem have little to do with being educated or uneducated.

Ranjit Singh was a devout Sikh. His daily work routine would start only after he had listened to a recitation from the Holy Granth. An elephant with a howdah of gold carrying the Guru Granth Sahib in it, invariably led all Ranjit's processions. So great was his faith in the Guru Granth that he never took any major decision or launched on an eminent undertaking without seeking its guidance. On occasions he would seek auguries from it even in trifling, minor matters. He was however, not a zealot or bigot.

The two biggest qualities by which the great maharaja was able to unite his people and succeed against heavy odds were to look upon all religions with one eye (respect for all faiths and religious tolerance) and his single-minded pursuit of power. He is known to have said, "God wanted me to look upon all religions with one eye that is why he took away the light from the other." He participated in the festivals of all faiths, he visited, prayed and made liberal donations to mosques and temples and there were no forced conversions in his time (the Sikh religion forbids proselytizing by coercion, bribe or exploitation); his Muslim and Hindu wives retained their faith; Moran (his Muslim wife) even caused a riot by converting a Hindu servant to Islam.

Alexander Burnes observed the religious tolerance and respect for all religions by the Sikhs. He remarked, 'The Seikh (Sikh) people are most tolerant in their religion; and I have remarked in India generally much more of this virtue than people give credit for.' – (*Travels in Bokhara, vol. II*). Dr Joseph Wolff, a Jew-turned-evangelist was also impressed with Ranjit's liberal views on religion and the futility of making forcible conversions. 'Randjud Singh has proved to the Mussulmans pretty well, that the edge of the sword is not always evidence of the truth of religion; for the name of Randjud Singh is a terror from Lahore to the city of Bokhara – his sword having defeated the Mohammedans in every battle.'

Ranjit Singh was a monarch of a secular state. His government was known as **Sarkar-e-Khalsa** because it belonged to the entire Khalsa. His kingdom was ruled through his subjects Hindu, Muslim and Sikh alike. They were chosen men of talent and ability, who controlled Ranjit's civil administration and the army. Merit, efficiency and loyality were the only consideration/criteria of his selection and not caste, creed or religion. Ranjit Singh made no discrimination on religious grounds and his court reflected the secular pattern of his state; it had a fine mix of Hindus, Muslims and Sikhs. His prime minister, Dhian Singh was a Hindu Dogra; his foreign minister, Azizuddin a Muslim and his finance minister, Dina Nath, was a Hindu Brahmin and likewise his army generals were Sikh, Hindu, Muslim and European Christians. These men remained loyal to him as long as he lived. The Austrian traveler Baron Charles Hugel remarked that the state established by Ranjit Singh was the most wonderful object in the whole world.

'He possessed the faculty, which is one of the highest attributes of genius, and for lack of which many brilliantly gifted men have suffered shipwreck – the faculty of choosing his subordinates well and wisely. He knew men, and he selected each servant for the special work which he could best perform, and consequently he was, even in a corrupt and violent age, wonderfully well served' writes Sir lapel Griffen, K.C.S.I. in his book 'Ranjit Singh' (page 92).

During his journey through the Punjab, one thing that struck Burnes was that there were very few Sikhs in the country. 'The paucity of Seikhs, in a country ruled and governed by them, is remarkable. The mother earth of the tribe is the Doab between the Ravi and the Sutlej, but there are few of them to be found thirty miles below Lahore, where they are said to predominate. There are no Seikhs westward of the Hydaspes (Jhelum); and to the eastward of Lahore, where they are said to predominate, they certainly do not compose a third of the population.' What did not come to his mind was that the Lahore kingdom was a Punjabi state and belonged to all Punjabis, Hindus, Muslims and Sikhs alike and the Sikh Maharaja ruled with the help of all of them.

Maharaja Ranjit Singh possessed a cool head – a quality very rare amongst hot-headed Punjabis. He never let anger cloud his judgment. Ranjit Singh was not impulsive or impetuous and never took hasty decisions in anger. Before taking a decision, he let his temper cool down; he asked for advice from his courtiers but followed his own judgment. He had patience and acted on his knowledge of human behavior and not on bravado.

Throughout his life, the Maharaja epitomized what a ruler should be, humble and always available for service to his people. Ranjit Singh was a docile and modest man, his government was Sarkar Khalsa ji, his Court Durbar Khalsa ji and his title was given to him by that mystic entity Panth Khalsa ji. The coins that he struck were named *Nanak Shahi* (of the emperor Nanak) coins and did not bear his name or effigy. He refused to sit on a throne or wear an emblem of royalty on his simple turban. He wore the plainest of clothes, saffron-coloured cashmere in winter and plain white muslin in summer. But he insisted that his courtiers and visitors wear all their finery (regalia and jewellery) in the Durbar. Ranjit Singh was entirely free from pomp and show, yet the studied respect of his court was remarkable; not an individual spoke without a sign though the throng was more like a bazaar than the court of the first native prince of India.

Capital punishment was unknown in Ranjit Singh's kingdom. Throughout his life he never passed a single sentence of death. He abolished the death sentence for every crime, however heinous it might be. Crime was generally atoned with fines. Fine (determined not according to the gravity of the crime but by the capacity of the criminal to pay) was the general mode of punishment and in criminal cases the punishment was quick and summary. 'Never was so large an empire founded by one man with so little criminality,' says Princep. 'Except in actual warfare,' writes Osborne, who visited him, 'he has never been known to take life, though his own has been attempted more than once, and his reign will be found freer from any striking acts of cruelty and oppression than those of many more civilized monarchies.' He built up a kingdom and a powerful army and yet he disliked bloodshed. Despite his many conquests, he did not allow any wanton destruction of life or property.

There is no doubt that such a leader of the caliber of Ranjit Singh was perforce loved and idolized by his people. The Aucklands saw something of the esteem in which Ranjit Singh was held by the people in the British protected part of the Punjab (i.e., Cis-Sutlej/Malwa or Sirhind region). At Ludhiana Lord George Eden Auckland (1784-1849), the Governor-General (1836-42) inspected howitzers which were to be presented to Ranjit. The guns had the star of the Punjab with Ranjit's profile engraved on them. The Governor-General's sister, Emily Eden, wrote in her diary: "Captain E. says that thousands of Sikhs have been to look at these guns, and all of them salaam to Runjeet's picture as if it were himself.' (Emily Eden, Up the Country, vol. I, p. 127). Emily Eden, who was with Ranjit Singh when they visited Amritsar wrote: 'There is something rather touching in the affection his people have for him. The other day, in going through the city, it struck us all, the eagerness with which they called out "Maharaja!" and tried to touch him, which is easy enough in these narrow streets, and the elephant's reaching the roofs of the houses.'

Doctor Honigberger, (1795 -1865) was physician to the court of Lahore from 1829 to 1849. In 1833, he suddenly became homesick and nothing could tempt him to remain. However, in 1838, on getting news of Ranjit Singh's critical illness he abandoned his practice, and rushed to Lahore. It was the Maharaja's generosity, the treatment meted out to him during his stay and respect and affection for the monarch that impelled him to return.

The Maharaja was a gifted ruler, with the natural genius of command. Men obeyed him by instinct and because they had no power to disobey. The control which he exercised, even in the closing years of his life, over the Sikh people, nobles, priests and the general public, was the measure of his greatness. What surprises historians is his total command and control over his kingdom and people even during the twilight years of his life. It was strange indeed to observe his complete ascendency over his brilliant court of fierce and turbulent chiefs, even when he had become feeble, blind, and paralysed.

Lt Henry Edward Fane was the young nephew of Sir Henry Fane, the Commander-in-Chief of the British Army. The subaltern accompanied the General to the court of Maharaja Ranjit Singh, as his ADC. Fane's account of his visit ends with a handsome tribute: 'Runjeet, among his subjects, has the character generally of a kind and generous master, and one of the best princes that has ever reigned in India. As evidence to his being a really good and amiable man, may be sited his kindness to children (two or three of whom he has crawling about the durbar), and the fact of his never having, since he conquered the country, put a man to death for even the most heinous crimes.' Regarding the Maharaja's love for children, Emily Eden says that the children of soldiers who had fallen in battle were always allowed in court. They were crawling about the floor, running in and out between Runjeet and the Governor-General.

'He has made himself a great King; he has conquered a great many powerful enemies; he is remarkably just in his government; he has disciplined a large army; he hardly ever takes away life, which is wonderful in a despot, and he is excessively loved by his people.', (Emily Eden in her book Up the Country, vol. I, pp198-9).

A captain Matthews, who had visited the chiefs of Malwa a month before the visit of Metcalfe and sent detailed reports on Ranjit Singh to the British described Ranjit Singh as 'a man of excellent understanding possessed of a most liberal, generous, friendly mind, untinctured with prejudices of any kind ...... The Rajah is not only a most unaffected and pleasing man in his manners but of a very good understanding, brave and liberal and seems to be quite the soldier and very fond of military exercises, but regrets that he can get no Europeans into his service ….He is both feared and believed by his men and frequently leads them on to the assault of forts; being a fatalist he says it is in vain for a man to screen himself and that what is to be his end must inevitably be so. He is the most capital horseman and rides every morning till 7 o'clock with only few attendants on the fine level plain between the walls of the town and the river, has beautiful horses some of which are from Iran and Kandahar, but the finest are bred in the country.' [1] SC 3 of June 20, 1808.

Dr Murray, was the British physician, sent to Lahore in 1836, by the English for treatment of Maharaja Ranjit Singh, after he had suffered a stroke of paralysis. His dispatches to the Ludhiana Political Agency provide information about the Maharaja, his government and his nobles. Murray writes about the splendour of Ranjit Singh's court, his fondness for his French officers, his regular inspection of troops, and the entertainment provided by his Zenana Corps. The doctor, observed that even when ill, the monarch invariably took an airing or went out for a ride. He held court where ever he happened to be. Everything, however trivial was brought to his notice, and he issued orders promptly on all matters. Murray is full of praise for the Sikh army.

Another important observation of Dr Murray was the Maharaja's inquisitiveness and fondness of long discourses. He made numerous enquiries about the composition of British European regiments, the Barrackpur mutiny, the siege of Bharatpur and various other military and administrative aspects. But, despite all this, the physician noticed that the Maharaja did not so much as mention an incident of insubordination which had occurred in the Sikh army camp near Lahore during his visit. Murray learnt about it from his servants, and felt surprised at his royal host's reserve in matters of State.

During Maharaja Ranjit Singh's reign, Sikh arms had attained their greatest power, the Sikh commonwealth its widest expansion and the Sikh religion had its prominence. It was *the Golden Period of Sikh History and the rising Sikh military power*.

Ranjit Singh was not a god. He had the virtues and faults of his people. And like the other contemporary kings of his time, he had human failings and vices, but similar to other great and renowned leaders his qualities far outweighed his weaknesses. The love of wine, women, horses, diamonds, and nautch girls remained with Ranjit Singh throughout his life, to the very end.

2

THE NIHANGS OR AKALIS

The Nihangs are a militant order among the Sikh people. The word Nihang is derived from the Persian *nihang* meaning crocodile, alligator, shark or water dragon, and signifies qualities of ferocity and fearlessness. They are also known as the reckless ones, though some say the word means naked. Originally Nihangs were suicide squads of the Mughal army and wore blue uniforms. The Sikhs took the name and the uniform from the Mughals. The order is said to have been founded by one of the elder sons of Guru Gobind Singh and it became very popular among the Sikhs. Nihangs, also known as Akalis (servitors of the timeless God), wear blue and dedicate their lives to the service of the community. Members of the present-day Sikh political party – the Akali party also wear blue turbans.

As mentioned, Nihangs are also known as Akalis. The word Nihang and Akali were synonymous. The term Akali means immortal, and the sect is so called because they are worshippers of the Immortal One or God Almighty. The Akalis are the only fanatical order of Sikhs and they are Khalsa or Govindi Singhs of the pronounced type. It is said that Guru Gobind Singh himself founded and organized this sect as a counterpoise to the Pathan Ghazi. Akali, a term now appropriated by members of the dominant Sikh political party, the Shiromani Akali Dal, founded in 1920, and groups splitting from it from time to time was earlier used for Nihangs (q.v.), an order of armed religious zealots among the baptized Sikhs (Khalsa).

While kingdoms were being lost and won around them, these dedicated soldiers of the Khalsa – "immortals" as they genuinely believed themselves to be – devoted themselves to the care of Sikh shrines. They had few needs and to serve a temporal master was against their creed. They were difficult men to get on with. Their whole way of life was a paradox. On the one hand they were humble and pious people continually praying and doing menial jobs for the love of the Guru in holy places and gurdwaras, on the other hand, they believed that they were entitled to exact from the community whatever they needed for their upkeep.

Before Mahaṛaja Ranjit Singh came to power; during the period of upheaval, when the *misls* (Sikh confederacies) were breaking up and Sikhs were at each other's throat, the Shahid or Nihang Misl was the only one of the twelve *misls* that kept aloof. The service of the Shahid or Nihang Misl was completely selfless, as the leaders of this *misl* did not occupy any territory. When fratricidal wars started among the Sikh *misls*, the Nihangs remained neutral, refusing to raise their weapons against fellow Sikhs. But whenever and wherever any *misl* faced a non-Sikh enemy, the brave men of this *misl* fought with unmatched valour and helped keep the Sikh flag (*Nishan Sahib*) flying high. After the battle they would always retire to their camps and immerse themselves in their religious duties.

Life in the open plains of Punjab, seasoned by constant riding and physical exercise had kept the Nihangs fit and more than aggressive. They lived in their *deras* or camps, where they performed their religious duties and practiced martial arts and horsemanship. They were equally apt at fighting on foot as well as on horseback. These men were tall and hardy, illiterate (they had knowledge of Sikh scriptures alright), excellent warriors and capable of moving at great speed and of enduring hardships that could decimate an army on foot. They were horsemen then and the remnants of them are horsemen today. Their equestrian skills were superb and even today they keep horses in their *deras* and their horsemanship is breathtaking.

Whenever there was any especially dangerous or bloody task to be done, or any difficulty to be overcome requiring courage and fearlessness to a very high degree, the Akalis were usually chosen to perform it. The Nihangs were fanatic bands of fighters who had since the times of Guru Gobind Singh formed the commando or suicide squads/troops of the Khalsa armies; they were employed on occasions when every other method proved futile and all was given up as lost. These men knew no fear. Only the fierce and warlike can dominate others. The Nihangs had won a name for valour and believed that they were invincible. They were, always under arms, the berserks of the clan went to battle as if they were going to a feast. They were dour and disciplined fighters, full of fire and dog like in their devotion to their religion and Guru. They were savage, wild, fierce, and tenacious with a lust for battle and made savage attacks. They were the flower of the Sikh armies. These people were an answer to the Muslim Gazis and the enemy dreaded them.

To give the Gazis a taste of their own kind of religious fanaticism, Maharaja Ranjit Singh used Akali Phula Singh and his band of Nihangs. The Akali character combined the best and the worst features of human beings. Their best quality was their dashing gallantry and their worst was blind fanaticism. The Sikh maharaja made use of both these qualities at the same time by throwing the Akalis into battle at critical moments in engagements against similar Muslim fanatics, for example, at Kasur and Nowshera. He owed many of his victories to the desperate valour of the Nihangs.

To serve a foreign master was against their tenets. In fact, it was a practice with them to be a little uncharitable to the powerful and the affluent. Like Robin Hood, it was an article of faith with them to defy and prey on the rich and influential while serving and helping the poor and the weak. While they were dreaded by the opulent and the privileged, they enjoyed a good deal of popularity among the Sikh masses. In the matter of religious doctrine and practice, they were uncompromisingly orthodox. According to Ali-ud-Din Mufti, the Akalis were an order that never cared about death and misery. And because of the respect for this order the Sikhs were strictly forbidden from oppressing these people or shedding their blood and doing so was a sinful act. The Akalis have, ever since their origin, been held in high esteem by the Sikhs. Their contingents were called the forces of Guru Gobind Singh. Therefore, they enjoyed the regard of the whole Sikh community. It was for this reason that the Shahid or Nihang Misl was held in deep veneration.

In the words of Gordan, "They exercised a fierce scrutiny as censors in upholding strict compliance with the militant creed of the Singhs (Khalsa), constituted themselves defenders of the faith against all innovations, took a prominent part in the councils in the planning and arranging of expeditions for averting national dangers and in educating the people in the doctrines of the Sikh religion." Through their extraordinary zeal and enthusiasm, they acquired the character of priests in which capacity they acted effectively while directing the conduct of the Sikh councils at the Akal Takht. They did not like the Europeans and Muslims because of their anti-Sikh practices. According to Malcolm they were, "insufferable to strangers for whom they entertain a contempt which they take little pains to conceal."

The Nihangs have a glorious past and during their heydays they were admired, respected and held in high esteem. They were long the dread, not only of their enemies, but of the other Sikhs too, and under Maharaja Ranjit Singh their power was very great. The *Nirmalas, Udasis, Sevapanthis* and *Nihangs* (or *Akalis*) were liberally endowed with grants of land by the maharaja, the Sikh chiefs and nobility. During the days of the Khalsa Raj, Maharaja Ranjit Singh gave the Nihangs a lot of concessions, perks and privileges, but **they refused to take any pay/remuneration for their services**. They were venerated, honoured and recognized for their daring deeds, chivalry and dauntless courage, but since the annexation of the Punjab the sect is declining.

Today, the Nihangs are still living in the past; they live in a world of their own, of past memory, not divorced from fantacy; their dress and lifestyle has not changed much. They live as they lived 300 years ago, in the same mould and in a time warp – same type of clothing, same type of weapons and attitude and they still maintain and ride horses. Even today, they are accomplished horsemen. In present times, the order has degenerated to a laughingstock. They are rigid adherents to the five K's prescribed by Guru Gobind Singh, but to show their absolute devotion to the sword, they supplement the 5 K's by carrying steel about their person to a very ridiculous extent. Nevertheless, they are a picturesque lot – the Sikh version of the Spanish author Miguel de Cervantes' **Don Quixote** with speech full of braggadocio.

A Nihang describes himself as a *Sava lakh* (equal to 125,000) or a *fauj* (army) in himself and calls his *dera*/camp a *chhauni* (cantonment). Similarly, they have colourful names for many items and actions. Coarse food like grams is *badam* (almonds); onions, ruppa (silver pieces); a chillie, ladaki (a quarrelsome dame); shoes/slippers, *athakksavari* (tireless mount); to die, *charhai karna* (an order to march out for an invasion/expedition) – and so on. This vocabulary was coined in the difficult days when the Sikhs suffered fierce persecution at the hands of the Mughal rulers. The jargon of hilarious euphemisms and humorous parallels to words and expressions in common use is indicative of high-spirited confidence and courage and how light they made of their adversity and mocked at their own misery and misfortune, in those dark days. This language was used to keep their morale and spirits high and to belittle articles of worldly comfort (beyond their reach) to the point of ridicule.

Today, Anandpur Sahib, the birthplace of the Khalsa, remains the main center of Nihang gatherings. They assemble here in their thousands in March every year to celebrate *Hola Mohala*, a Sikh festival introduced by Guru Gobind Singh. On that occasion, they display their martial and equestrian skills and hold competitions (in the use of traditional weapons) and mock battles. The most spectacular part of the festival is the magnificent procession of Nihangs on horses and elephants and on foot in their typical costumes carrying a variety of traditional and modern weapons and demonstrating their expertise in using them. Crowds throng at Anandpur, the media, journalists and foreigners from all over the world come to watch the Nihangs, to shoot them with their cameras and make films on them.

The names of some famous Nihangs are Baba Deep Singh (1682-1757), the founder of the Shahid misl and Damdami Taksal (school of Sikh learning) - he fell fighting at the Golden Temple, Amritsar, Nihang Gurbakhsh Singh (of village Khem Karan, who along with thirty Sikhs pounced on the army of Abdali at the Golden Temple and attained martyrdom), Akali Naina Singh (guardian and tutor of Akali Phula Singh), Akali Phula Singh (*jathedar* of Akal Takht and commander of Maharaja Ranjit Singh's crack Akali brigade), Nihang Natha Singh, Nihang Hanuman Singh and Akali Kaur Singh Nihang (1886-1955), a scholar and religious preacher and some others.

- The Nihangs and Akalis were identical till the middle of the nineteenth century, when the Sikh political supremacy was extinguished in Punjab. A political party known as the Akali Dal was formed on 14 December 1920. The Akali Dal launched the Gurdwara Reform Movement (aka Akali movement) in 1922. **This was when the Akalis and Nihangs really began to be considered as separate entities**.

A paragraph from Rudyard Kipling's book '**KIM**' (Page 71-72, Chapter IV) reads as follows:

Then an Akali, a wild-eyed, wild-haired Sikh devotee in the blue-checked clothes of his faith, with polished quoits glistening on the cone of his tall blue turban, stalked past, returning from a visit to one of the independent Sikh states, where he had been singing the ancient glories of the Khalsa to College-trained princelings in top-boots and white-chord breeches. Kim was careful not to irritate that man; for the Akali's temper is short and his arm quick.

3

HOW THE SIKHS BECAME SARDARS

According to the encyclopedia of Sikhism, *Sardar*, in Persian is amalgam of *sar* (head) and *dar* (a suffix derived from the verb dashtan, i.e., to hold) meaning holder of headship, is an honorific signifying an officer of rank, a general or chief of a tribe or organization. During the Guru period (1469-1708) and for half a century thereafter, no words indicative of high rank was current among the Sikhs other than the common appellation *bhai* or, rarely *baba* to express reverence due to age or descent from the Gurus. Later the Sikhs adopted the title of sardar for the leaders of their *jathas* or roving bands fighting against Afghan invaders under Ahmad Shah Abdali or Durrani. With the expansion of the fighting force of the Sikhs under the *misls* (Sikh confederacies) the number of Sikh sardars multiplied. During the Mughal and British period **sardar** was a coveted title officially conferred on generals or civil officers of rank.

The eighteenth century was a very significant and crucial period for the Sikhs. After the death of Guru Gobind Singh (07 October 1708), the enmity between the Sikhs and the Mughal State became fiercer. A partially successful rebellion (1709-1715) by Banda Singh Bahadur against the Mughal rulers of the Punjab was followed by a period of brutal persecution of the Khalsa Sikhs. The Mughal governors were butchers of the Khalsa. They served an evil and brutal regime and during the Mughal rule and Afghan invasions, they persecuted the Sikhs ruthlessly, with savage barbarity. The subsequent history is a tale more of suffering than of visible triumph. It was a period of continuous but sporadic fighting between the two adversaries; both parties displayed an implacable enmity and a bloodthirsty spirit of revenge. Every advantage that the ruling Delhi regime gained over the Sikhs was followed by terrible and brutal retribution. Despite all the disadvantages the Sikhs were not slow to retaliate whenever the fortunes of war favoured them. At one time the Mughal persecution (slaughter) of the Sikhs was so great that it seemed the Sikhs had almost ceased to exist and for a few years very little was heard of them. Hunted out of their homes, the Sikhs scattered in small *jathas* or groups to find refuge in wild, inaccessible and uncharted country - distant hills, forests and deserts, but they were far from vanquished.

During this dark period, the Sikhs, living as outlaws in jungles and deserts began to reconsolidate and prepare for the future. Despite the inhuman cruelties inflicted on them by the Mughals, the Sikhs survived due to their humour, enthusiasm, religious fervor and unity of purpose and living. That indomitable and resolute spirit which Guru Gobind Singh had done his best to instill into his followers, allowed no defeat to crush or cow them. In their adversity, they kept their spirits high and remained cheerful and merry by all kinds of means at their disposal. They cut jokes and coined their own jargon (the slangs are still in use by the Nihang Sikhs, even today). Throughout the course of this melancholy, depressing and disheartening time when everything seemed lost; the Khalsa sang *Raj karega Khalsa*, in order to raise their morale. Guru Gobind Singh had conferred the sovereignty of the land on the Khalsa. The Sikhs literally claimed it as a boon granted them by their Guru; and in this manner it is claimed to have received divine sanction. The Sikhs were impelled by the weight of tradition that had grown up with the period of time, that it was the destiny of the Sikhs to rule (*Raj Karey ga Khalsa*). They acknowledged no earthly superior and implicitly believed that:

The Khalsa shall rule.
Their enemies (non-believers) will be scattered.
Only they that seek refuge will be saved.

Fortunately for the Sikhs they had an ally in the ferocious bigotry of Emperor Aurangzeb which created enemies to his throne in every feudatory Hindu state, and eventually brought the magnificent fabric of empire to the ground. As to the Sikhs, his persecutions strengthened their obstinate attachment to their faith, and the threat of death and torture never won Islam a single convert. Then there followed a period of chaos and confusion; in this period of turmoil the Mughal Empire was hastening to its fall and gradually became weaker and weaker, breaking up through its own inherent rottenness as well as by the attacks of its enemies and foreign invaders. Ironically, it was historical justice that the very people Aurangzeb sought to destroy, destroyed the Mughal rule in India.

Nadir Shah invaded India in 1739 and this was followed by the nine raids of Abdali between 1747 and 1767. Ahmad Shah Abdali was an Afghan of the Saddozai clan and Nadir Shah's most trusted general. On his master's assassination, he usurped power and became ruler of Afghanistan under the title of *Durrani* (from *dur-i-dauran*, the best of pearls). During each invasion the Sikh guerillas harassed him and lightened his burden by stripping him of some of the booty that he was carrying home to Afghanistan and, also rescuing the captives that he was taking home as slaves. It was during these Afghan invasions (1747-1769) that the Sikhs started their upward ascent to power.

Abdali was the bitterest and most implacable foe of the Sikhs; he spilled more Sikh blood than any other of their enemies. But paradoxically he was the greatest benefactor of the Sikhs. His repeated incursions destroyed Mughal administration in the Punjab. During his fifth invasion, Abdali fought the third battle of Panipat (January 14, 1761), he routed the Marathas and gave them a crushing blow. It may not be wrong to say that this battle fought between the Marathas and Afghans was actually won by the Sikhs. Abdali taught the Sikhs that no people could become a great nation without shedding blood. He created a vacuum in Punjab which was filled by the Sikhs and he failed to put down the Sikhs because they refused to meet him on his terms. They seldom fought pitched battles but adopted hit and run tactics. Their lightening attack was bold and robust. The Sikhs raided his rear columns and vanished into to the hills and jungles as swiftly as they had come. When and where they would strike again there was no telling. They were everywhere and yet elusive; fighting the Sikhs was like slashing a sword in water. (Khushwant Singh - A History of the Sikhs)

These times were rife and favourable for the bold and restless spirits who, combining ability and ambition with courage were led to attempt great things for themselves. These daring and courageous, brave men gathered supporters and attempted to carve out kingdoms for themselves from the ruins of the Mughal Empire. Among the Sikhs the bolder spirits pushed forward as leaders, collected around them a following and began to attempt not only sovereignty and independence but empire. At the Baisakhi meeting of the *Sarbat Khalsa* (commonwealth of Sikhs) in 1748, the large number of *jathas* (groups or bands) was finally merged into twelve *misls* (Sikh confederacies) and it was resolved to merge the independent *misls* into one army the Dal Khalsa whenever the need arose. Hence, the *misls* were collectively known as Dal Khalsa (army of the Sikhs). The Dal Khalsa was to function under the unified command of Jassa Singh Ahluwalia.

During these years of struggle against the Mughals and Afghans the Sikhs evolved a constitution peculiarly their own. Every Sikh looked upon himself as a **Sardar** (chief), the only organization he was willing to accept was one in which his independence and equality was granted. Every *misl* was free to act in any way it wished in the area under its influence or control, and every Sikh was free to join any *misl* he chose. Thus, there was liberty, equality and sovereignty on both sides i.e., the *misl* as well as the Sikh warrior. Only in matters affecting the community as a whole were they to combine and take orders from the Supremo, Jassa Singh Ahluwalia. The strength of the *misls* varied from time to time. It is estimated that the total strength that the Dal Khalsa could muster was about seventy thousand horse and foot.

The *misldari* system worked well under leaders like Nawab Kapur Singh and Jassa Singh Ahluwalia. It ideally suited the times and conditions that prevailed. It combined freedom of action with the discipline of a unified command. Most importantly it channeled the energies of the wild and fiercely independent Khalsa soldier in the service of a cause that he dearly espoused – the banishment of aliens from the soil of the Punjab and the accomplishment of the prophecy of their Guru of the establishment of a Khalsa state.

Mir Manu, (the governor of Punjab) died in May 1754. The *Dal Khalsa* with its headquarters at Amritsar emerged as the strongest force in the province. In the winter of 1754-55 Sikh horsemen swept through Ambala and Sirhind and later into territory that is known as Haryana today and onwards into the kingdom of Jaipur. Punjab had no government and the people were devoid of security of life and property. This reality dawned on the Khalsa and, they offered them protection (*rakhi*). *Rakhi* (protection) was, like the *chauth* of the Marathas, a levy of a portion, usually one-fifth of the revenue assessment of a territory, as a fee for the guarantee of peace and protection.

Rakhi (protection cess or tax) amounting to one-fifth of the produce was collected at the end of each harvest. Since the Sikhs were the only authority that had the power to fulfill its obligations, most of the Punjab accepted this offer of protection. This was the first step taken by the Sikhs towards becoming real sardars and rulers of the country. Hereafter for all practical purposes the country came to be administered by the Sikhs. It was during this period of time that the word **Sardar** for all the Khalsa Sikhs came into vogue in the true sense; initially only the heads/leaders of the jathas (roving bands) which later combined to form *misls* were called **sardars**.

After the death of Mir Manu (governor of Punjab), Jassa Singh started seizing villages and towns that were thrown into confusion by the state of chaos that followed. In September 1761, a combined force of Jassa Singh and some other Sikh *misls* overpowered the troops of Khwaja Ubaid Khan, Governor of Lahore and then besieged and occupied Lahore. Jassa Singh Ahluwalia was proclaimed King of Lahore and he declared the **sovereignty of Sikhs**. In January 1764 the Dal Khalsa under the command of Sardar Jassa Singh Ahluwalia conquered Sirhind. With this victory the whole country from the Indus to the Yamuna was functionally at the mercy and control of the Sikhs and the Sikh leaders immediately set about partitioning it between themselves. Thus far the *misls* continued to be autonomous, with freedom to enhance their hold and levy *rakhi* over any area they chose.

Gradually by 1767 the complete territory between the Indus and the Yamuna fell absolutely into the hands of the Sikhs. As soon as a battle was over, horsemen galloped madly in different directions claiming village after village by the simple act of leaving a personal token like a turban or a shoe to mark their ownership. He went on doing so, day and night, until he was famished and almost naked. Another method followed was that the horseman would first demand money from the *Zamindars* (landlords) of the village through which he passed. If no money was forth coming, he would ask for *gur* (jaggery/coarse sugar). And if even this was not available, he would take some bread (*chapattis*). The horseman would then depart and visit other places. But the Sikh horseman soon returned. Taking those petty offers as tokens of submission of the villagers', he would establish his sway over every village through which he had ridden. After this the various chiefs or **sardars** (big and small) of the Dal dispersed and then set out on fresh conquests in a similar fashion. The country was thus partitioned off and occupied by the Sikhs. The Khalsa Sikhs now came to be called **Sardars** and they also addressed each other as Sardarji.

Adversity, unity of purpose and a common enemy had kept the Sikh *misls* united. Now that there was no danger from abroad and plenty of land to appropriate, the *misl* organization began to lack cohesion. This period saw the breakup of the *misls*. The only reason why men continued to owe allegiance to some *misl* or the other was to safeguard their own possessions or add to them. As soon as they reached the limit prescribed by foreign powers, they had no option but to turn against each other. The *Sarbat Khalsa* (commonwealth of Sikhs) became a serpent with many heads. Thus divided, the Sikhs could not contend effectively with the Afghans, the Marathas, or the English who were also operating in the area.

An apt picture of the time is given by Imamuddin Husain Shahi and H. R. Gupta. "In the country of the Punjab from the Indus to the banks of the Yamuna there are thousands of chiefs in the Sikh community. None obeys the other. If a person owns two or three horses, he boasts of being a sardar (chief), and gets ready to fight against thousands. When a village is besieged by the Sikhs to release tribute which the Zamindars cannot afford, they intrigue with other Sikhs and the Sikhs begin to fight between themselves. Whoever wins receives money according to the capacity of the villagers." (Imamuddin Husain Shahi, 242-43; H. R. Gupta, II, 19-20)

George Foster gives an account of the awe and respect with which the people treated the Sikhs at the time. "I saw two Sicque (Sikh) horsemen, who had been sent from their country to receive the Siringnaghur tribute which is collected from the revenues of certain custom-houses. From the manner in which these men were treated, or rather treated themselves, I frequently wished for the power of migrating into the body of a Sicque for a few weeks – so well did these cavaliers fare. No sooner had they alighted, then beds were prepared for their repose, and their horses were supplied with green barley pulled out of the field. The *Kafilah* travelers were contented to lodge on the ground and expressed their thanks for permission to purchase what they required; such is the difference between those who were in, and who were out of power." - Forster, 1, 326.

An English traveller, William Forster, who witnessed the *misl* squabbles for power wrote in 1783: "Should any future cause call forth the combined efforts of the Sikhs to maintain the existence of empire and religion, we may see some ambitious chief led on by his genius and success and absorbing the power of his associates, display from the ruins of their commonwealth the standard of monarchy." The person about whom these prophetic words were written was no other than Ranjit Singh of the Sukerchakia *misl*. He overpowered all the other *misls*; tamed the wild and fierce Sikhs and their haughty and wayward ways and forged the mighty, magnificent and glorious Sikh empire.

During the rise of Sikh *misls* and when the Sikhs attained political power at the time of Sikh rule (reign of Maharaja Ranjit Singh and his successors), the title **sardar** came to be used more rampantly as an appellation for all Sikhs in general having Singh as their common surname. Later the British government also used the word selectively by incorporating it in the titles of *sardar sahib* and *sardar bahadur* conferred mostly, but not exclusively on Sikhs.

In order to summarize, we observe that initially only the heads/leaders of the *jathas* (roving bands) which later combined to form *misls* were called **sardars.** The word **sardar** for all Sikhs came in vogue when the Khalsa started their upward ascent to power and became more assertive. The term **Sardar** for all Khalsa Sikhs gained more currency in 1761, when the Sikhs occupied Lahore and Jassa Singh Ahluwalia declared the sovereignty of Sikhs. Subsequently the Sikhs started levying *Rakhi* (protection) tax from the people and the title of **sardar** became even more common for them. Ultimately, it was when the Sikhs became the virtual masters of the complete territory between the Indus and the Yamuna; gained political power and were the only power and authority that mattered, that the epithet of **sardar** was consummated and deeply embedded for all Khalsa Sikhs. But this had its maladies too. Adversity, unity of purpose and a common enemy had kept the Sikh *misls* united. Now that there was no danger, the *misl* organization began to lack cohesion and breakup. The awe and respect with which the people treated the Sikhs at the time made them haughty and arrogant. The Sikh commonwealth lay in ruins and many a golden opportunity that could have been availed with the strength of combination and a common cause was thrown to the winds.

The Sikhs became sovereign, gained power and self-esteem and became arrogant and high headed. Their ego knew no bounds and each of them was a chief (sardar) in himself. Equality, liberty and sovereignty were very dear and close to a Sikh's heart. All this had not come easily; it had been gained over a long period of time through vicissitudes, trials and tribulations; they had undergone privations, suffering, persecution and sacrifice. It had been won with the sword and not begged or borrowed from anyone. Therefore, each Khalsa Sikh was a **sardar**; he was called a **sardar**; he behaved like a **sardar** and he deserved the title. Though, the times are once again changing but generally, every turbaned Sikh with unshorn hair is addressed as *sardarji*, and it is customary to use *sardar* in place of "Mr" before a Sikh name.

Even within the borders of each confederacy itself, the barons were always quarrelling and first one chief and then another took the lead. **This was due to the constitution of Sikhism, under which no such thing as vassalage or feudal superiority was acknowledged. The principle of the creed was fraternity, and the Sikhs boasted of being communities of independent soldiers.**

- Sir Lepel Griffin, K.C.S.I.

4

HOW SIKHS LOST THE IMPERIAL CITY OF DELHI

Also known as Dilli, the capital of India is steeped in history. Delhi is also connected with Sikh history. The first, sixth, eighth, ninth and tenth Gurus visited the city and the two wives of Guru Gobind Singh (Mata Sundari and Mata Sahib Devan) stayed here for a long time before and after the death of the Guru. There are historical Gurudwaras in Delhi to commemorate these events. A Sikh *sangat* existed in what came to be known as Kucha Dilvali Singhan in Old Delhi.

Banda Bahadur stormed Sirhind and entered the town on 24 May 1710. His next big conquest was Saharanpur; he invested the town after crossing the Jumna River and ruthlessly plundered it. Panic spread in the Jumna-Gangetic Doab. The sight of one Sikh lancer on horseback was enough to terrorise a whole village. The only power that mattered and commanded respect was that of Banda Bahadur and his peasant armies. In those fateful days, had Banda shown more enterprise he could have **captured Delhi** and Lahore and changed the entire course of Indian history. But it was not to be. The otherwise daring Banda showed a lack of decision and this proved fatal to his dreams.

After the crumbling of the Mughal Empire and the rise of Sikh power in the Punjab during the last three decades of the eighteenth century (*Misl* Period), the *misl* armies of the *Dal Khalsa* extended their hegemony and levied *rakhi* or tribute in many towns and villages in the Jumna-Gangetic Doab. They operated right up to the walls of Delhi. The Mughal court of Shah Alam II was in a dilemma. Najaf Khan (the ablest and right-hand man of the emperor) soon realized that neither the Mughals nor the Marathas were strong enough to deal with the Sikhs.

The Sikhs got many a chance to enter and capture Delhi, but time and time again they did not bother to avail of these lucrative opportunities. They **spared the imperil domains; including Delhi** and let these chances slip through their fingers **even when the road to Delhi was rolled out for them like the proverbial red carpet**. All that it required was a bold chieftain to lead his troops into the capital city of Delhi, take the emperor under his protection, and without any effort make the Sikhs the greatest power in all Hindustan. But not one of the Malwa Sardars showed the courage or wisdom to take this step. They appeared and reappeared in the neighbourhood of **the imperial city and, instead of capturing it**, went further on to create havoc.

On one occasion Jassa Singh Ramgarhia penetrated into the heart of Delhi and carried off four guns from the Mughal arsenal. He is also known to have uprooted and carried to Amritsar a red granite slab on which the Mughal Emperor Aurangzeb sat and gave orders of execution of Sikhs. **This granite slab, today, lies on the roof top, above the langar of the Golden Temple, Amritsar (the Ramgarhia Bunga)**.

In January 1784 over thirty thousand horsemen under the leadership of Jassa Singh Ramgarhia and Karam Singh crossed the Jumna and began to collect *rakhi* from the towns and villages between the two rivers. These Sardars, who dared so much in the field of battle showed surprising timidity in the political arena; when invited by the emperor **they shied away from taking the Imperial city under their protection**. The emperor was left with no choice; he perforce had to turn to the Marathas and English for help.

The Sikhs *misls*, the English, the Marathas and the Rohillas, all had their vested interests. The struggle for the possession of the Jumna-Gangetic Doab (land between two rivers) went on for six years and on several occasions the Sikhs crossed the Ganges and the sordid game of ganging up sometimes with one, sometimes with the other went on. The Maratha agent in Delhi reported candidly: **"The Emperor rules inside the city, while outside the Sikhs are supreme."**

All along the English guarded their personal interests. They made all efforts to prevent the Sikh chiefs from making any friendly connections with the Marathas. In 1803 the British occupied Delhi (**Bhanga Singh, the Sikh chief of Thanesar had joined hands with Lord Lake in attacking Delhi in September 1803**). When Lord Lake entered Delhi in 1803, he was shown a miserable blind old imbecile, sitting under a tattered canopy. It was Shah-Alam, 'King of the World,' but captive of the Marathas, a wretched travesty of the Emperor of India. He had been blinded by Ghulam Qadir (son of Rohilla chief Zabita Khan) on 10 August 1788. Ghulam Qadir had entered the imperial city with the help of a *jatha* (roving band) of Sikhs under Bhagel Singh and let loose a reign of terror. The British, now the rulers of Delhi, fixed an annual pension for the Emperor, Shah Alam II. **Henceforth, the Sikhs could never ever think of occupying Delhi even in their wild dreams**.

The above incidents proved to be the degradation of the misls and also the undoing of the Sikhs and their unique institution, the Dal Khalsa. Sir Lepel Griffin, K.C.S.I., author of the book *Ranjit Singh* (page 77) says, "Thus the Sikhs, both by their defeat and by their victory, acquired a status, which they did not before possess, and

had they known how to put aside private jealousies and unite habitually as they had done for the conquest on Sirhind, they would have become as formidable and irresistible in North India as the Marathas in the South and West. But the democratic nature of the Sikh faith, responding to the natural sentiment of the people, resisted all attempts at dictation by one central authority, until Maharaja Ranjit Singh broke down opposition and reduced rivals and enemies to a common obedience."

The silver lining in the dark cloud of the sad drama that ensued in Delhi and its suburbs was the construction of historical Gurdwaras in Delhi. **Between 1765 and 1783, the Sikhs conquered Delhi fifteen times**. In March 1783, the Sikhs overran Delhi and captured the Red Fort; they ransacked Malka Ganj and Sabzi Mandi and actually **entered the Red Fort on 11 March 1783**. Sardar Baghel Singh Krorsinghia (*jathedar or* leader/commander of the Krorsinghia Misl) unfurled the Kesri (saffron) flag on Red Fort. Hindus, Sikhs and Muslims willing joined his procession from Red Fort to Fatehpuri. The Sikhs established their supremacy over Delhi.

The helpless Mughal Emperor Shah Alam II sought mediation by the Muslim turned Christian lady Begam Samru of Sardhana and came to terms with the Sikhs. The Sardars fell to the charms of the petite lady. Five Sikhs (including Sardar Jassa Singh Ahluwalia and Sardar Baghel Singh) accepted the entreaty of Begum Samru and agreed to leave Delhi but retained the right to raise memorials to their Gurus. They agreed to retire with the main force provided Sardar Baghel Singh of Karosinghia Misl was permitted to stay in the capital with 4,000 men till the construction of gurdwaras on sites of historical importance to the Sikhs was completed. Some Sikh historians emphatically write that by withdrawing from Delhi, the Sikhs proved that their desire to serve their Gurus was more than their desire to rule Delhi (this is a cover up for the follies of the Sikhs).

Sardar Baghel Singh got the gurudwaras built in Delhi. To meet the expenses, Bhagel Singh was authorized to charge six *annas* in a rupee (37.5 per cent) of all income from octroi duties in the capital. During his stay in Delhi from March to December 1783, Bhagel Singh located seven sites and constructed gurdwaras on them. One gurdwara, Nanak Piao, existed earlier and another one Damdama was constructed later. Mosques had been built on the sites of Gurdwaras Sis Gang, Rikab Gang and Bangla Sahib which the Sikhs demolished. The nine historical gurdwaras of Delhi are:

1. Nanak Piao – near Azadpur where, Guru Nanak got a well dug and established a booth to serve water to wayfarers.

2. Majnu Tilla – here Guru Nanak taught Majnu the importance of selfless service to mankind rather than austerities. Guru Hargobind also stayed here.

3. Bangla Sahib – close to Connaught Place. It was the mansion or *bangalow* of Mirza Raja Jai Singh, where the eighth (boy) Guru Har Krishan stayed during his visit to Delhi.

4. Bala Sahib – where the infant eighth Guru Har Krishan and the wives of Guru Gobind Singh (Mata Sundari and Mata Sahib Devan) were cremated.

5. Sis Ganj – the site of execution of the nineth Guru Tegh Bahadur in Chandni Chowk.

6. Rikab Ganj – the site of cremation of the ninth Guru Tegh Bahadur near Parliament House in New Delhi. The Sikhs had to demolish a mosque built twice on this site.

7. Moti Bagh – located on the Ring Road near Dhaula Kuan. Guru Gobind Singh set up camp here on his arrival at Delhi in 1707.

8. Damdama Sahib – near Humayun's tomb on the outer Ring Road in New Delhi where a meeting between Guru Gobind Singh and Bahadur Shah (later Emperor) took place sometime in May-June 1707

9. Mata Sundri – the site of the residence of the two wives of the tenth Guru (Mata Sundari and Mata Sahib Devan) from 1729 till their death. It is located at Kucha Dilvali Singhan in Old Delhi.

This article will not be complete without a mention of Sardar Baghel Singh (d. 1802) of the Karosinghia Misl. In 1765 Baghel Singh succeeded Karora Singh as leader/chieftain of the Karosinghia Misl. Sardar Baghel Singh was a Dhaliwal Jat and belonged to village Jhabal in Amritsar district. He became a formidable force in the cis-Sutlej region; the Mughals, Rohillas, Marathas and the English sought his friendship and in Sikh history he is known as the vanquisher of Mughal Delhi.

Sardar Baghel Singh first invaded Delhi on 08 January 1774 and captured the area up to Shahdara. The second invasion was on 17 July 1775, when the Sikhs captured the area around the present-day Pahar Ganj and Jai Singhpura. Most of the fighting took place where present day New Delhi is located. Shortage of supplies forced the Sikhs to temporarily halt their conquering spree. Finally, on 11 March 1783, the Sikhs entered the Red Fort in Delhi and occupied the Diwan-i-Am (Audience Hall for Commoners). The Mughal Emperor Shah Alam II reconciled with the Sikhs, made a treaty and agreed to their terms and conditions. Sardar Baghel Singh stayed in Sabzi Mandi, with 4,000 troops, and took charge of the police station in Chandni Chowk while the gurdwaras were being constructed from April to November 1783.

Not many know that even today, Delhi stands witness to this chivalrous act of Sardar Baghel Singh. The place where Bhagel Singh stopped with his troop of 30,000 soldiers in Delhi is known as **Tees Hazari**. The Mughal emperor had closed all the gates of the Red Fort. The Sikhs accidentally came across a mason, who showed them a spot where the wall of the fort was weak because it had caved in from inside, but the exterior was intact. The Sikhs broke into the Red Fort from this place and occupied the Diwan-i-Am. This place, located where the Inter-State Bus Terminus now stands, is now known as **Mori Gate**. After acquiring the Red Fort, the Sikhs distributed sweets and this place is now known as **Mithai Pul**.

ALL YOUR STRENGTH IS IN YOUR UNION
ALL YOUR DANGER IS IN DISCORD.

- H W Longfellow, *Hiawatha*

5

THE THREE QUISLINGS

The decade following the exit of the benevolent ruler of Punjab is the sad and sordid narrative of the follies and crimes of the nobles. As long as he lived, Maharaja Ranjit Singh knew how to deal with the British and they knew how to tackle him. If he was cautious of the British, they too knew his strength and the loyalty of his subjects. But as soon as he died, everything turned topsy-turvy, his kingdom was in turmoil. The throne founded by genius was surrounded by a crowd of greedy, unscrupulous parasites, who had no thought but of enriching themselves at the expense of the people. There were factions (The Court, Dogra brothers and Sandhanwalia sardars), conspiracies, intrigues, treasons and murders and the princes, ministers and sardars were engulfed in this bloody carnage. The Sikh kingdom was lost by the infidelity and treachery of some of her own people. Discipline and obedience gave way to conspiracy and revolt; enthusiasm was succeeded by contempt; till the dynasty was extinguished amidst the laughter of those who had applauded its birth.

The British set spies and traitors to work to create conditions favourable for a successful occupation of the country. A number of the Maharaja's top officers fell prey to temptation and sided with the British. They had turned betrayers and deceivers. They were Tej Singh (a Gaur Brahmin turned Sikh from Meerut district), Lal Singh, a Brahmin of Sanghoi in Jehlum district of West Punjab - now Pakistan, the European officers, the Hindustanis (Poorbias employed in the Durbar's forces), the Dogra brothers, and the Sandhanwalia Sardars. They were jackals in the lair of lions. **The Fakir brothers and Raja Dina Nath were perhaps the only people who remained loyal to the Lahore Durbar**. The three main and most prominent quislings were Tej Singh, Lal Singh and Gulab Singh Dogra. They were among the foremost of the whole lot of back-stabbers and informers. These three deceivers and turncoats played the leading role in the ruin of the Sikh Kingdom.

Tej Singh, Raja (1799-1862), was son of Misr Niddha, a Gaur Brahman of Meerut district. His original name was Tej Ram and he was the nephew of Jemadar Khushal Singh (a man of inferior ability and degraded habits). He (Tej Singh) took up service at the court in 1812 and in 1816 received the rites of Khalsa and became Tej Singh.

The size of the Maharajah's household and visitors to the court had increased enormously and he was in the need of a *deorhidar* (Royal Chamberlain or keeper of the royal palace). His choice fell on a handsome youth from Meerut called Khushal Chand, who had enlisted as a common soldier. Khushal Chand was promoted to the rank of *Jemadar* and then placed in the new appointment. It gave the incumbent political power as well as a handsome income from presents. After accepting the Sikh faith, he came to be known as Jemadar Khushal Singh. Jemadar Khushal Singh introduced two relations of his to the court; a younger brother, Ram Chand (Ram Singh after becoming a Sikh) and a nephew, **Tej Singh**. It was this Tej Singh who, after the death of the Maharaja, played a treacherous role as commander of the Sikh armies in the first Anglo-Sikh war.

This family of Brahmins exerted a baleful influence on the Lahore Durbar. It was one of the rare instances of Ranjit Singh misjudging the quality of the men he employed. Tej Singh proved his worth as a soldier and made rapid progress in the army rank structure, becoming a general in 1818. He took part in many campaigns. On the eve of the First Anglo-Sikh War (1845-46), Tej Singh was appointed commander-in-chief of the Sikh army. His conduct during the war and the one following was however marked by duplicity. He proved to be shameless, cunning and unscrupulous – a traitor of the worst kind. He established secret liaison with the British and desired their victory rather than that of the army he led, thus clandestinely betraying the Sikh forces.

Two divisions under Tej Singh's command hovered around Firozpur when the strategic town could have been stormed and the small British garrison destroyed. At the fiercely fought Battle of Ferozeshah (21 December 1845), he kept the army away from the battlefield. When the action was over, he appeared with his army on the morning of 22 December 1845 and drove straight into the shattered British cavalry lines. But suddenly his guns ceased firing and he abandoned the battlefield and retreated towards Lahore. At Sabhraon (10 February 1846), he advised the brave and loyal Sikh general, Sham Singh Attariwala, to flee the battlefield. But Sardar Sham Singh was undeterred; he stood his ground and continued the fight until he fell fighting against heavy odds. The two coward commanders, Tej Singh and Lal Singh took to their heels even as the contest hung in the balance.

Tej Singh fled across the pontoon bridge as soon as the contest started and had it destroyed, making reinforcements and retreat of the Sikh army impossible. In such a situation, the result of the battle was a foregone conclusion. Such were the generals of the Sikh army, who got their own troops murdered. They were willing to sell out the Punjab provided their lives and *jagirs* were secured and they fulfilled their treacherous promises to the English. At the end of the war, he made an offer of Rs. 25,00,000 to Lord

Hardinge to buy for himself an independent kingdom like Gulab Singh had done. The British did not fulfill Tej Singh's desire, but in order to drive home the correct message to future traitors, they did not forget the services rendered by the crafty Tej Singh to the British Empire. He was allowed to retain all perks, privileges and rights and his position of pre-eminence in the new set-up. Over and above, he was given more prestigious offices, posts and ranks and made Raja of Sialkot in August 1847. During the mutiny of 1857, Tej Singh raised Sikh cavalry regiments to aid the British. His scattered *jagirs* (estates) were consolidated and he received the new title 'Raja of Batala'. He died on 04 December 1862 and was succeeded by his brother, who was also his adopted son Harbans Singh, before the birth of his own son, Narinder Singh.

Gulab Singh (1792 - 1857). In due course of time Kushal Singh was removed from the post of Chamberlain and in his place was appointed Dhian Singh Dogra – a man of great charm and courtesy. The Dogra introduced two other brothers in the court. The elder, **Gulab Singh**, was a smooth-spoken man. The younger, Suchet Singh, who was appointed conveyer of petitions, was in addition to his native courtesy, strikingly handsome. The year (1818) marked the beginning of the ascendancy of the Dogra family in the affairs of the Lahore Durbar.

The Dogra brothers, who were upstarts, became within nine to ten years the most powerful element in the Lahore Durbar. Their father, Mian Singh, had been made a raja and given his home province, Jammu as a *jagir*. Gulab Singh (1792 -1857) was the eldest son of Mian Kishora Singh Dogra. He joined Maharaja Ranjit Singh's army in 1809 as a trooper on a daily allowance of three rupees. He won the approbation of the Maharaja and rose in rank and status. The family's fortunes suddenly rose when his father, Kishora Singh was made the chief of Jammu in 1820 by the

Maharaja. In 1822, on the death of his father, Kishora Singh, the title was conferred on Gulab Singh. Gulab Singh was a fine soldier and he served his master well in various campaigns. The official Lahore diarist, Sohan Lal Suri, has recorded the bounties and favours bestowed upon him by the Maharaja from time to time. Financially, he was the most highly favoured vassal and tributary of the Sikh state. As long as the Maharaja lived, Gulab Singh remained loyal, humble and subservient to him and relied more on his brother, Raja Dhian Singh, to promote the interests of the family.

After the death of Maharaja Ranjit Singh, the wily Gulab Singh started misappropriating revenue and wealth. His intrigues against the Lahore government, so infuriated the Khalsa army that in 1845, a strong force had to be sent to Jammu, in order to chastise him. Machiavellian in character, Gulab Singh was cunning, shrewd and unscrupulous. He was a wolf in sheep's clothing; a silent operator. The British countenanced him as a force countervailing the Sikhs. Gulab Singh retained liaison with the British and passed military intelligence to Brigadier Wheeler at Ludhiana on the eve of the First Anglo-Sikh War (1845-46). When the British were trying to destroy the Sikh rulers, Gulab Singh, their principal commander sat silent and did not help to save the Sikh Kingdom. Gulab Singh stopped sending supplies and rations from Lahore during the war and, also prevented the Dogra troops from joining the Punjabis on the battlefield. Obviously, the British had to reward him for the secret assistance that he had rendered them.

Raja Gulab Singh was invited by the Governor General at a camp on March 15, 1846. Following this Raja Gulab Singh was bestowed with the title of a Maharaja and the Treaty of Amritsar (16 March 1846) was signed between the British and Maharaja Gulab Singh. As a result of this treaty, Maharaja Gulab Singh found himself in possession of the State of Jammu and Kashmir. Jammu and Kashmir was sold to Gulab Singh Dogra for a sum of Rupees 75 lakh. This was part of the Sikh territory, ceded at the end of the war, to the British by the treaty of Lahore (9 March 1846). Gulab Singh also became, according to another article of this treaty, a vassal of the British, whose supremacy he acknowledged.

As the British were keen to get rid of the volatile Sikh threat to their Empire, hence, they found that the best strategy was to stick with Raja Gulab Singh. The Sikh Kingdom was weakened by depriving it of valuable territory and reducing its army. This Treaty of Amritsar marked the beginning of Dogra rule in Kashmir, which was to end in 1948, after an attack by the Pakistani army, led to the Indo-Pakistan War of 1947. Lord Hardinge gave the following reason for the transfer of Jammu and Kashmir to Maharaja Gulab Singh, "It was necessary last March to weaken the Sikhs by depriving them of Kashmir."

The battle of Gujerat (21 February 1849) was a disaster to Punjabi arms from which they could scarcely hope to recover. The coup de grace was, however, delivered by the arch-traitor, Gulab Singh Dogra. He helped Abbot to cut off Sher Singh Attriwala's retreat towards the frontier. The prospect of continuing the fight with Afghan help was thus obviated. He also arranged for supply of boats for the British army to cross the Jhelum. Sher Singh tried to negotiate terms but the British insisted on an unconditional surrender.

HARDING PAPERS are private and public correspondence and public dispatches of Lord Harding, Governor General of India (1844-48), relating to the Punjab and Sikhs regarding the First Anglo-Sikh War (1845-46). They relate to **Gulab Singh's overtures to the British Government**, terms imposed on the

Sikhs, and the stripping of one-third of Sikh territory (to weaken Sikhs) by making it over to Gulab Singh. Gulab Singh was to be independent of the Sikhs and rule over Jammu and Kashmir.

Harding never fully trusted Gulab Singh: "I am rather discreet and moderate.... I rather like diplomacy, when regulated by integrity.... The man, whom I have to deal with, **Gulab Singh, is the greatest rascal in Asia**.... We can protect him without inconvenience and give him a slice of Sikh territory which balances his strength in the same degree against theirs; and he is geographically our ally, I must forget that **he is a rascal** and treat him better than he deserves."

Gulab Singh died at Jammu on 30 June 1857. It may be of interest to the reader to know that today, Nirvan Singh (grandson of Punjab Congress chief minister Amarinder Singh, a scion of the erstwhile Patiala royal family) is married to Mriganka Singh, granddaughter of senior Congress leader Karan Singh, a Rajya Sabha MP and scion of Jammu and Kashmir's princely family. The marriage was solemnised with Sikh and Hindu rituals on Saturday 04 March 2017, in the presence of their grandparents and other close family members and relatives.

Lal Singh, Raja (died 1866), son of Misr Jassa Mall, a Brahmin shopkeeper of Sanghoi, in Jehlum district of West Punjab, entered the service of the Sikh Darbar in 1832 as a writer in the treasury. Gradually Lal Singh rose to power and he increased his influence by winning the favour of those in authority. Lal Singh was a disloyal and selfish man; he worked through subterfuge; he owed loyalty and allegiance to none save himself. In fact, he was a master strategist, player of secret hands and seizer of chances, expert in a world of power and danger where victory goes to the most cunning. He turned against his patrons one by one, when his ends were served, and it suited his self-interest and purpose to oppose them. To this end, in 1843, Lal Singh engineered the murder of Beli Ram, his own benefactor, and Bhai Gurmukh Singh. He displayed similar ingratitude to Dhian Singh and his son Hira Singh.

By his beguiling manner Lal Singh won the confidence of Maharani Jindan Kaur and became her closest adviser. She appointed him a member of the Council of Regency (December 1844) and a Wazir (minister) on 8 November 1845. As Wazir and as a commander, Lal Singh proved disloyal to the Sikh Darbar in the first Anglo-Sikh war of 1845-46. He acted in conformity with the secret instructions received from the British officers. He supplied military secrets and information to Captain Peter Nicholson, at Firozpur, and two divisions of Sikh troops under his command remained entrenched at Ferozeshah without attacking Firozpur. Brigadier Littler's garrison troops were thus allowed to escape from there and form junction with Lord Cough's army at Ferozeshah. After the reverse at Ferozeshah, Lal Singh fled post-haste to Lahore and offered the Council of the Khalsa to relinquish his office. He was relieved of the office of Wazir, but no change in the military command was made.

On the eve of battle of Sabhraon (10 February 1846), Lal Singh is alleged to have sent to Captain Nicholson a map of the Sikh entrenchments. During the battle, he deliberately kept his artillery regiments and the dreaded *Ghorcharas* (cavalry) away from the battlefield and himself retired to Lahore. After the war, he was suitably rewarded by the British. He was confirmed as Wazir of the State of Lahore under the Resident, Henry Lawrence. He, however, lost British patronage when it came to light that he had sent written instructions to Shaikh Imam Ud-Din, the governor of Kashmir, to thwart the occupation of the valley by Gulab Singh. Jammu and Kashmir had been granted to Gulab Singh by the British, vide the

Treaty of Amritsar (16 March 1846). Lal Singh was tried by a Court of Inquiry and found guilty. He was removed from his high office and expelled from Punjab with a pension of Rs. 12,000 per annum. He was sent to Agra and then to Dehra Dun. Lal Singh lived in Dehra Dun and Mussoorie till his death in 1867.

Perhaps, history will never find a better example of such dastardly intrigue and treachery, where greedy and ungrateful leaders and generals were hell-bent upon destroying their own innocent, faithful and patriotic soldiers. Both the Sikh commanders Lal Singh and Tej Singh, Raja Gulab Singh Dogra, many of the chieftains, both Sikh and Dogra and the Europeans were in secret treasonable communication with the English and in all probability Rani Jindan Kaur (the widow of Maharaja Ranjit Singh) was aware of it. These men (deceivers, lip servers and sycophants), the Khalsa had so trustingly patronized and raised consequently to the highest civil and military offices proved to be traitors, and betrayal and duplicity characterized them. They arranged massacres of the invincible Khalsa armies for personal gain.

The Sikh soldiers (simple, loyal and credulous) were defeated not by British skill but by chicanery and the treason of their leaders. In the war with the British, the naïve, illiterate, and gullible Sikhs were misled to destruction by their treacherous leaders and generals. The Sikh soldiers displayed the utmost gallantry in vain. A proper appreciation leaves no doubt that even according to the admissions of responsible adversaries; the Sikhs defeated the British in each and every engagement.

The Sikh Kingdom fell because of one single simple reason and that is 'the people were unfit.' The nobility had endured wealth too long; they had been softened by luxury; luxury was their only enemy. Everything had been presented to them on a platter. They could not perceive the value of what they had got.

"Easy Come, Easy Go"

The wily, shrewd and corrupt quislings were not ashamed of their dastardly deeds. They were all crafty, shameless, cunning and unscrupulous people, who knew how to play dirty with no remorse or regret. The Machiavellian British never felt guilty or embarrassed of such an ignoble, dishonorable, immoral, and cowardly victory, won by fraud. They were fair weather friends and lip servers. The British government exploited the situation to their advantage to the complete ruin of their less fortunately placed friend and ally, and yet proclaimed to the world that they had been themselves grossly wronged. The Christian (a religion of love) values and British honour and justice that the English so often, boast of and preach to the world had vanished. In fact, it had been transformed into British intrigue, betrayal and duplicity. But then it is said, "Everything is fair in love and War." It is correctly said, 'Ends justify the means.' and 'All nations work on self-interest.'

6

HOW THE STATE OF JAMMU AND KASHMIR WAS FORMED

Maharaja Ranjit Singh had always wanted to make Kashmir a part of his kingdom, two earlier attempts to conquer Kashmir had failed. Hardly a month had passed after the victory at Attock when his mind turned to Kashmir again. And, once an idea entered his head it could not be dislodged. Ranjit captured Peshawar and then made earnest and concerted arrangements to seize Kashmir. The information of the Maharaja's preparations for war was conveyed to Azim Khan, the Afghan Governor of Kashmir, who dispatched his agents to solicit help from the English. Sir David Ochterlony, the agent to the Governor General at Ludhiana Political Agency (1809 - 14), who had received advance instructions on the subject, told them that his government could not consider it and explained that the British Regime was bound by treaty not to interfere in the affairs of the regions west of the Sutlej and dismissed the Kashmir envoys.

By April 1819 the snows had melted, the passes to the vale of Kashmir were open. The Maharaja had decided to make his third attempt to conquer the valley. This was the right opportunity to wrest Kashmir from the Afghans because Azim Khan, despite his diplomatic failure at Ludhiana took a chance in leaving Kashmir for Afghanistan to avenge the murder of his brother, Wazir Fateh Khan. He left his younger brother Jabbar Khan with a force he considered adequate to defend the valley. Agar Khan, the chief of

Rajauri, who was in Lahore swore on the Quran (or Koran) to help Ranjit in every way he could. Moreover, in an earlier campaign in the north-west, Maharaja Ranjit Singh had snapped all connection between Kashmir and the western hinterland of Afghanistan and the Pathan tribal territory, so there was little danger of any sizable force coming from those quarters to oppose him. Everything seemed propitious.

The Sikh army concentrated at Wazirabad, the headquarters for the Kashmir operation. Fearing a call for 'Jihad' by the Afghans, Ranjit Singh did not forget to bring Akali Phula Singh and his band of Nihangs along. The forces were divided in three, one was to form the reserve and stay with the Maharaja at Wazirabad, the second led by Misr Diwan Chand and third under Prince Kharak Singh. The latter two were to proceed together as far as Rajauri and then they were to split and make a pincer movement on Shupaiyan, where they expected to encounter the enemy, Afghan troops. All logistics (supplies and munitions) and operations were to be directed from the headquarters at Wazirabad.

After the two columns left for Rajauri, the Maharaja received secret and confidential information that Agar Khan was likely to defect. He took pre-emptive measures to avert the danger and ordered the release of Sultan Khan, Chief of Bhimbar (who had been in prison for seven years), offering to reinstate and reward him if he undertook to guide the Lahore soldiers over the Pir Panjal range. Ranjit Singh was correct in his judgement of the two men. As soon as the first skirmish took place between the advance columns of the Durbar and the Afghans, Agar Khan deserted to the enemy and the Sikh army had to rely on Sultan Khan of Bhimbar.

Kharak Singh's column advanced without much opposition up to Baramgulla and, guided by Sultan Khan, was able to side-track the Poonchis and reach Shupaiyan. Meanwhile, Diwan Chand, after crossing the mountains had to force his way through due to casualties inflicted by Pathan snipers. The two columns were able to marry up on the battle field where Jabbar Khan's 12,000 Afghan troops stood in battle array on the plain of Shupaiyan.

Diwan Chand let his troops rest and recoup for a few days, then he suddenly and swiftly surrounded the Afghan host. In the wee hours of the morning of 03 July 1819, Durbar batteries opened fire on the Afghans. Not having as many guns as the Punjabis, Jabbar Khan ordered his cavalry to charge. Enemy horsemen captured many guns. Akali Phula Singh gave signal to his Nihangs to enter the fray. The Afghan cavalry and infantry could not stand the Nihang blitz, they recoiled and scattered. The Sikhs had won a decisive victory and the coup de grace had come from the Akalis. News of the victory reached the Maharaja the next day whilst he was marching up to reinforce his troops. Thus, the Sikhs became the masters of Kashmir, they ruled Kashmir for 25 years (1819 - 46) with their own governors.

The great Sikh Maharaja died on 27 June 1839. As soon as Maharaja Ranjit Singh died, everything turned topsy-turvy, his kingdom was in turmoil. There were factions, conspirations, treasons and murders and the princes, ministers and sardars were engulfed in the bloody carnage. The decade following the exit of the benevolent ruler of Punjab is the sad and sordid narrative of the follies and crimes of the nobles. The throne founded by genius was surrounded by a crowd of greedy, unscrupulous parasites. These ungrateful quislings, sycophants, hypocrites and traitors had been brought up on the crumbs of the Maharaja.

The **1809 Treaty of Lahore** between the British Government and the Maharaja of Lahore was ratified on 30 May 1809. **It was a treaty of perpetual friendship and peace between the two powers**. But the English were not bound by their treaties. They were only bothered about colonial expansion, hegemony and imperialism. For the British, ends justified the means and they used all weapons in their arsenal to achieve this. They intentionally created situations, provoked rebellions and designed favourable conditions and circumstances for a takeover and then cried being the prey and victim. This has been amply brought out by John Sullivan in his book *'Are We Bound by Our Treaties?'*

It was an invariable custom with the English, first to gain a footing by the excitement of avarice, by the promise of assistance or other flattering terms, and then by gradual steps to assume the government of the country. The British were unscrupulous schemers, skilled in the craft of giving graft and corrupting the locals. They bribed and depraving the ministers and other officials. They were past masters in the art of intrigue, subversion, deceit and the use of spies and fifth columnists. Their spy system was perfect and functioned continuously; in moments of crisis and in the heat of war there would be defections in their favour which made a great difference. They won most of their battles before the actual fighting took place.

The result of Machiavellian British policy was the **First Anglo-Sikh War (1845-46).** Five battles were fought – Mudki (18 December 1845), Ferozshahr (21 December 1845), Baddowal (21 January 1846), Aliwal (28 January 1845) and Sobraon (10 February 1846). From the beginning the aim of the leaders of the Sikhs was the destruction of the Sikh army, which had become too strong for the inept and weak successors of Ranjit Singh and the Lahore Durbar to control and manage. Both the Sikh commanders Lal Singh and Tej Singh, Raja **Gulab Singh Dogra**, many of the Chieftans, both Sikh and Dogra and the frangees employed in the army of the Sikhs were in treasonable communication with the

English and in all probability Rani Jindan (the widow of Maharaja Ranjit Singh) was aware of it.

The wily Dogra Gulab Singh had been in league and seditious contact with the British. He gave away military secrets and helped the English in all ways sought by them and fulfilled his part of the promise to them. He stopped sending supplies and rations from Lahore and prevented the Dogras from joining the Sikhs. Time and again, valuable time was lost. Hesitation and indecision (whether by design or default) of the generals marred Sikh action and military operations. It was a criminal blunder against all principles of war. This crucial and unpardonable lapse gave the English enough time to rest, recoup and more essentially for their reinforcements to fetch up. How could such an army confront the enemy?

The Sikh soldier proved his worth and mettle again and again during the Anglo-Sikh Wars and emerged unblemished. He was however let down badly by the infidelity of his leaders. They were lions being led by sheep. They fought with nothing but sheer raw courage and made savage, dare devil, and fierce attacks. The soldiers were not allowed much tactical fighting. They were driven into the jaws of death and became fodder for the guns. The Sikh soldiers were sitting ducks at the guile and mercy of the enemy. They lost more men in these grave circumstances; in excess of what they would, in fair and rightful warfare. What an unjust disadvantage!! Never the less the Sikh soldier was great and noble and did not flee from the battlefield. He went down fighting with grace, honour and dignity. The result of the war was a foregone conclusion. They were literally uncontested battles and were lost before they had begun or the first round was fired.

The Anglo-Sikh War is a narration of corruption, lost victories, strategic opportunities that beckoned and were missed and the heart-breaking story of bright prospects turning to ruin. The battle accounts and a close scrutiny leave no doubt that even according to the confessions of responsible adversaries, the Sikhs trounced the British in each and every encounter. Perhaps, history will never find a better example of such dastardly intrigue and treachery, where greedy and ungrateful leaders and generals were hell-bent upon destroying their own innocent, faithful and patriotic soldiers. The Sikh soldiers (simple, loyal and credulous) were defeated not by British skill but by chicanery and the treachery of their leaders.

After the First Anglo-Sikh War the traitors were rewarded by the English for their infidelity and ignoble and dastardly services that they had rendered them and the *sardars* who had dared so much in the field of battle, showed surprising timidity in the political arena; they were brilliant leaders in war, but incapable of handling the reigns of civil government. They requested the wily traitor Raja Gulab Singh to negotiate for them. This suited the British because he was their stooge and would do their bidding. The British took over the Punjab and a caretaker government was installed, vide the treaty of Lahore on 09 and 11 March 1846 and ultimately a fresh Treaty of Bharowal on 16 December 1846. In order to undermine and supress the Sikhs, the British sold Jammu and Kashmir (J & K) to the traitor Gulab Singh for 75 lakh rupees and recognized him as Maharaja of J & K.

Lord Hardinge (1844-48), the *tundalat* (one-armed Lord) had already made up his mind about the future of the Sikh kingdom. He knew that there were still far too many Khalsa soldiers scattered about in the country to permit annexation; so, he contended himself with terms which would facilitate a take-over at a more appropriate time. The Sikh Kingdom was weakened by depriving it of valuable territory and reducing its army.

Having conquered the entire land and achieved what they wanted they exploited their subjects and made them dance to their tune at their own sweet will and wish. After the First Anglo Sikh War (December 1845 - February 1846) the British took over Punjab and installed a caretaker government. The Sikh Kingdom was debilitated by devesting it of precious territory and drastically reducing its army. Lord Hardinge gave the following reason for the transfer of Jammu and Kashmir to Maharaja Gulab Singh, **"It was necessary last March to weaken the Sikhs by depriving them of Kashmir"**.

Harding Papers are private and public correspondence and public despatches of Lord Harding, Governor General of India (1844-48), relating to the Punjab and Sikhs regarding the First Anglo-Sikh War (1845-46). They relate to **Gulab Singh's overtures to the British Government**, terms imposed on the Sikhs, and the stripping of one-third of Sikh territory (to weaken Sikhs) by making it over to Gulab Singh. Gulab Singh was to be independent of the Sikhs and rule over Jammu and Kashmir.

Harding never fully trusted Gulab Singh: "I am rather discreet and moderate.... I rather like diplomacy, when regulated by integrity.... The man, whom I have to deal with, **Gulab Singh, is the greatest rascal in Asia**.... We can protect him without inconvenience and give him a slice of Sikh territory which balances his strength in the same degree against theirs; and he is geographically our ally, I must forget that **he is a rascal** and treat him better than he deserves."

The British were keen to get rid of the volatile Sikh threat to their empire and felt that the best strategy for this was to stick with Raja Gulab Singh. Eventually Raja Gulab Singh was invited by the Governor General at a camp on 15 March 1846. Following this Raja Gulab Singh was bestowed with the title of a Maharaja and the Treaty of Amritsar was signed between the British and Maharaja Gulab Singh on 16 March 1846. As a result of this treaty Maharaja Gulab Singh found himself in possession of the State of Jammu and Kashmir. The Treaty of Amritsar marked the beginning of Dogra rule in Kashmir, which was to end in 1948 after an attack by the Pakistan army that led to Indo-Pakistan War of (1947-48).

This is how the kingdom (princely state) of Jammu and Kashmir was created after the First Anglo-Sikh War, from the territories that had earlier been in the erstwhile Sikh Empire and Gulab Singh was eventually made the Raja of J and K by the treaty of Amritsar dated 16 March 1846. In 1947, at the time of independence of India J and K opted to be independent. It was a state with a Hindu ruler and Muslim population. The Dogra rule in Jammu and Kashmir lasted for a century (1846 - 1948). A list of the Maharajas of Jammu and Kashmir is appended:

Gulab Singh (1846 - 56)

Ranbir Singh (1856 - 85)

Partap Singh (1885 - 1925)

Hari Singh (1925 - 52) – Monarchy abolished in 1948

Karan Singh (!952 - 61) - Titular

Some rise by sin, some by virtue fall

7

THE BETRAYAL OF SIKHS

Neither as leaders nor as a community had the Sikhs played any noteworthy part in Indian national politics before 1947. They had neither the training nor the experience to cope with the problems of partition. Unversed in national politics, divided in their attitude towards the British – the Sikhs reverted to the historical posture of communal defence and defiance. The powers-that-were in the central governance of India complained of the political incompetence of the Sikhs.

The Sikhs were fooled and deceived by the Congress and during the rioting at the time of partition, the Congress high command put the Sikhs in the forefront and encouraged them to kill, loot, murder and burn. They called Sikhs the 'sword arm of Congress.' In reality they wanted the Sikhs to destroy themselves as a separate effective community which may at some time become a source of trouble to them.

The Sikhs knew that the best way to get concessions was to use the 'Khalistan' card. Even though they knew the strength of their case, Congress ensured that they did not press or persist in their demands. Every community is entitled to the right of self-determination. Sikhs lacked political wisdom. Eventually the Sikhs did not get Congress support for the establishment of Khalistan. The Congress did their job well in inciting and exploiting the Sikhs, leading them to the eventual destruction of their identity. The Sikhs are simple people who act before they think. They were the worst hit. They lost all their rich agriculture land, property and holy shrines (gurudwaras) in West Punjab which became Pakistan and to add to all this was the suffering and loss of life during the mass scale exodus from Pakistan. They could have had an independent/semi-independent state of their own if they had played their cards well.

At the time of partition of India in 1947, the leaders of the Indian National Congress (INC), in particular Mahatma Gandhi and Pundit Jawahar Lal Nehru assured the Sikhs that they would be given a semi-autonomous State in the Punjab. All the volumes of the "*Transfer of Power Documents*" reveal that the British did their best to persuade the Sikhs to ask for a separate independent state. Putting blind faith in the assurances of the Congress leaders, the Sikhs did not listen. The Congress leaders were masters at the art of perfidy and by subtle chicanery they beguiled the Sikhs and betrayed them later. The gullible and credulous Sikh leaders were no match to the subterfuge of Mr Nehru. They had been assured repeatedly that the Congress would not let down the Sikhs in any constitutional arrangements for the independence of India.

For example, as far back as 1929, at the annual session of the INC, held that year at Lahore, which was presided over by Jawahar Lal Nehru, the following resolution was passed:

"The Congress assures the Sikhs that no solution in any future Constitution of India will be acceptable to the Congress that does not give them (the Sikhs) full satisfaction."

(A. C. Banerjee: Indian Constitutional Documents, Vol. II. p. 317)

Again in 1931, while addressing a meeting of Sikhs at the Sis Ganj Gurdwara in Delhi, Mahatma Gandhi told the Sikhs:

"I ask you to accept my word and the resolution of the Congress that it will not betray a single individual much less the Community of Sikh friends. You have no reason to fear that it (the Congress) would betray you. For, the moment it does so, the Congress would not only thereby seal it's on doom but that of the country too."

Mahatma Gandhi went on to say:

"Moreover, the Sikhs are a brave people. They know how to safeguard their rights by the exercise of arms if it should come to that. What more can I say than this: let God be witness to the bond that binds me and the Congress with you. In case of betrayal, the Sikhs would in that case take their kirpans (sabers) in hand with perfect justification before God and man."

(*The Young India*, March 19, 1931).

In 1946, at the Congress Committee session at Calcutta, Mr Nehru said:

"The brave Sikhs of the Punjab are entitled to a special consideration. I see nothing wrong in an area and set-up in the North wherein the Sikhs can experience the glow of freedom. Redistribution of provincial boundaries is essential and inevitable. I stand for semi-autonomous units. If the Sikhs desire to function in such a unit, I would like them to have a semi-autonomous unit within India so that they have a sense of freedom."

(New Cambridge History of India, p. 205, The Statesman, Calcutta, 7 July 1946)

In March 1946, when the British Cabinet Mission arrived in New Delhi, they met the Sikh leaders, Master Tara Singh, Giani Kartar Singh, Harnam Singh and Baldev Singh. Members of the Cabinet Mission asked the Sikh leaders to *"specifically express their views on whether they favoured a united India, or its division, and in the case of its division, whether they would join India or Pakistan, or would they like to have a state of their own."* The Sikh spokesman, Master Tara Singh, said that they were for a separate Sikh state with the right to federate either with India or Pakistan. Giani Kartar Singh elaborated the latter alternative as a *"province of the Sikhs where they would be in a dominant position."* The Congress Working Committee on learning this quickly passed a resolution assuring the Sikhs *"of all possible support in removing their legitimate grievances and in securing adequate safeguards for the protection of their just interests in the Punjab."* In response, the Sikhs abandoned their demand for a separate Sikh state and threw their lot with the Congress which resulted in Baldev Singh joining Nehru's interim Government as Defence Minister on 2nd September 1946.

(New Cambridge History of India, pp. 176-177)

In a resolution moved by Mr Nehru on 9th December 1946, in the Constituent Assembly, Nehru said:

"Adequate safeguards would be provided for minorities in India. It is a declaration, pledge and an understanding before the world, a contract with millions of Indians and therefore in the nature of an oath we must keep."

(B. Shiva Rao: Framing of the Indian Constitution – A Study, p. 181)

Even as late as 5th January 1947, at the Congress session at Delhi, the Congress leaders again publicly repeated assurance of its support to minorities, particularly the Sikhs.

In April 1947, Mr Jinnah, in consultation with certain most powerful leaders of the British Cabinet in London, offered, to the Sikhs, first through Master Tara Singh and then through the

Maharaja of Patiala, a sovereign Sikh state, comprising areas lying to the west of Panipat and east of the left bank of the river Ravi, on the understanding that the state would confederate with Pakistan on very advantageous terms to the Sikhs. Master Tara Singh summarily rejected this attractive offer and the Maharaja of Patiala declined it after consulting Sardar Patel and Pundit Jawaharlal Nehru.

(Are Sikhs a Nation? p. 99)

On the 17th of May 1947, Lord Mountbatten, Pundit Jawaharlal Nehru, Nawab Liaqat Ali Khan and Sardar Baldev Singh, flew to London on the invitation of the British Cabinet, in search of a final solution to the Indian communal problem. When the Congress and the Muslim League failed to strike any mutual understanding and Pundit Nehru decided to return to India, the British Cabinet leaders conveyed to Sardar Baldev Singh that if he stayed behind, arrangements could be made *"so as to enable the Sikhs to have political feet of their own, on which they may walk into the current of world history."* Baldev Singh promptly divulged the content of this confidential offer to Pundit Nehru, and in compliance with the latter's wishes, declined to stay back. He flew back to India after giving the following brave message to the press:

"The Sikhs have no claims to make on the British except the demand that they should quit India. Whatever political rights and aspirations the Sikhs have, they shall have them satisfied through the goodwill of the Congress and the Hindus."

(Are Sikhs a Nation? p. 101)

In a bid to reinforce these commitments, the Congress Working Committee passed yet another resolution in March 1947 regarding the scope of the Constituent Assembly jurisdiction. It was specifically mentioned therein that no Constitution would be imposed on people of any State without their consent and approval. *It is relevant to point out that even till date, the Constitution of India has not been formally accepted by the Sikhs for failure of its founding fathers to honour their commitment with the Sikhs. The then, two Sikh members of Constituent Assembly Sardar Hukam Singh and Sardar Bhupinder Singh refused to sign it.*

Immediately after independence of India, the Sikhs were unashamedly betrayed by the Indian National Congress. They were deceived and denied the promised *"Semi-autonomous Unit"* in Punjab. The Congress reneged on their solemn promise which Nehru had described as *"a contract"* and *"in the nature of an oath"*; the promises on which the Sikhs had acted by opting for India and rejected Jinnah's very tempting offer of a sovereign state federated with Pakistan. J. N. Sahni, the veteran editor of the *Hindustan Times* wrote, *"The letting down of the Sikhs was not an act of carelessness on the part of the Congress leaders, nor even a blunder, but an act of gross and unpardonable betrayal."*

In 1947, when the Sikh leader Master Tara Singh reminded Nehru of the solemn promises made to the Sikhs by Congress leaders, and of his speech in Calcutta a year earlier, Nehru replied, *"the situation is different now."* The Sikh leader was branded *"an extremist"* and imprisoned for demanding a measure of autonomy for the Sikhs.

Master Tara Singh was not the only one to clash with Nehru on the issue of an autonomous state for the Sikhs. Hukum Singh, who later became the Speaker of the Indian Parliament, was a member of the Constituent Assembly which drafted the Constitution of free India. He walked out of the Assembly when he found that the Congress leaders were going back on their assurances to the Sikhs, and later all the four Sikh members of the Constituent Assembly refused to sign the Assembly's Report. Hukum Singh had the guts to call Nehru a cheat. He is on record as having made the following statement:

"Pundit Nehru is, to say the least, the spearhead of militant Hindu chauvinism who glibly talks about nationalism, a tyrant who eulogises democracy and a Goebbelian (i.e., like Goebbels, Hitler's Minister of Propaganda) liar – in short a political cheat, deceiver and double-dealer in the service of Indian reaction."

(Amritsar, p. 38)

Sikhs, who keep reminding the Congress leaders of the broken promises are readily branded as secessionists, traitors and troublemakers, when in truth it is the double-dealing Congress leaders like Nehru and Patel who are the real culprits, who treacherously betrayed the Sikhs.

It is the reneging of the Congress leaders on solemn promises made to the Sikhs, followed by equally grave injustices, such as the diversion of Punjab's water and hydro-power resources to neighbouring states – a death blow to Sikh farmers, which is the root-cause of the trouble in Punjab. The Indian Government has divided the Punjabis along communal lines and successfully carried out propaganda that Sikhs are terrorists, anti-national and separatists. They even went to the extent of making Punjabi the second language of Punjab. The Punjab problem has been very accurately assessed by Dr. Madanjit Kaur of Guru Nanak Dev University:

"The present generation of the Sikh community is facing a problem of discontent, and is in direct clash with the State which has been evading basic issues of the Punjab problem for decades and instead has been following a policy of tyranny, suppression and

violation of human rights by introducing draconian laws, extra-judicial measures, illegal detention in police custody, locking in jail without trials and eliminating the Sikh youth in false encounters."

(Professor Madanjit Kaur in *Co-existence in a Pluralistic Society*, p. XIV)

Sikhs can never tolerate injustice and tyranny. It is their ideology (given by their religion) to fight the two. History gives evidence that they are not going to easily forget what is rightfully theirs. The issue for an autonomous State will keep raising its head till it is satisfactorily addressed.

Mahatma Gandhi called Guru Gobind Singh, "a misguided patriot." In 1950 Patel called the Sikhs a *zalim kaum* (cruel community) and made Punjabi the second language of Punjab. Many more demeaning things were said against the Sikhs and the Sikh fight for freedom was subtly converted into the 'Freedom struggle of India.' Perhaps, they were unaware of history and the circumstances under which the Sikhs were being persecuted and the Mughals were trying to convert the whole of India to Islam. The irony is that both of them did not live to see the year - 1962 and Mr Nehru's death was hastened by the Chinese aggression.

It may not be out of place to quote a paragraph from the last statement (WHY I KILLED GANDHI) that Nathuram Godse made before the Court on 5th of May 1949. Such was the power and eloquence of this statement that one of the judges, G. D. Khosla, later wrote, *"I have, however, no doubt that had the audience of that day been constituted into a jury and entrusted with the task of deciding Godse's appeal, they would have brought a verdict of 'not Guilty' by an overwhelming majority."*

"-----------------In fact, honour, duty, and love of one's own kith and kin and country might often compel us to disregard non-violence and to use force. I could never conceive that an armed resistance to an aggression is unjust. I would consider it a religious and moral duty to resist and, if possible, to overpower such an enemy by use of force. [In the Ramayana] Rama killed Ravana in a tumultuous fight and relieved Sita. [In the Mahabharata], Krishna killed Kansa to end his wickedness; and Arjuna had to fight and slay quite a number of his friends and relations including the revered Bhishma because the latter was on the side of the aggressor. It is my firm belief that in dubbing Rama, Krishna, and Arjuna as guilty of violence, the Mahatma betrayed a total ignorance of the springs of human action. In more recent history, it was the heroic fight put up by Chhatrapati Shivaji that first checked and eventually destroyed the Muslim tyranny in India. It was absolutely essential for Shivaji to overpower and kill an aggressive Afzal Khan, failing which he would have lost his own life. In condemning history's towering warriors like Shivaji, Rana Pratap and Guru Gobind Singh as misguided patriots, Gandhiji has merely exposed his self-conceit. He was, paradoxical as it may appear a violent pacifist who brought untold calamities on the country in the name of truth and non-violence, while Rana Pratap, Shivaji, and the Guru will remain enshrined in the hearts of their countrymen for ever for the freedom they brought to them. ----------------"

In his Journal dated 1 February 1948, Lord Wavell, architect of Indian independence during 1943-47, records, "Gandhi wrecked the May 16, 1946 Plan which might possibly have secured a united India and saved all the massacres. I do not believe that he really worked for an understanding with the Muslims when his influence might have secured it. He was always the lawyer and the *Bania* (trader) who would drive a hard bargain and then find a legal quibble to deprive his opponent of what he had seemed to gain."

- Pg 288 – Fragments of Half a Century by Karnail Singh

The bane of the Sikhs has always been poor leadership and this time too their leaders let them down very badly.

Until the lions have their own historians, the history of the hunt will always glorify the hunter.

- Chinua Achebe.

8

Did India get Freedom because of Gandhi

When BP Chakravarti was acting as Governor of West Bengal, Lord Attlee visited India and stayed as his guest for three days at the Raj Bhavan. Chakravarti asked Attlee about the real grounds for granting Independence to India.

Towards the end, I asked Lord Attlee about the extent to which the British decision to quit India was influenced by Gandhi's activities. On hearing this question Attlee's lips widened in a smile of disdain and he uttered, slowly, putting emphasis on each single letter "*mi-ni-mal.*"

This 'unimpeachable' truth will come as a shock to most Indians brought up to believe that the Congress movement driven by the 'spiritual force' of Mahatma Gandhi forced the British to leave India.

But both the evidence and the logic of history are against this beautiful but childish fantasy; it was the fear of mutiny by the Indian armed forces - and not any 'spiritual force'- that forced the issue of freedom. The British saw that the sooner they left India the better for themselves, for, at the end of the war, India had some three million men under arms. Majumdar had reached the same conclusion years earlier, as far back as 1948 as he records. The most dramatic event after the end of World War II was the INA Trials at the Red Fort — not any movement by Gandhi or Nehru. This led directly to the mutiny of the naval ratings, which, more than anything, helped the British make up their minds to leave India in a hurry. They sensed that it was only a matter of time before the spirit spread to other sections of the armed forces and the rest of the Government. None of this would have happened without Subhas Bose and the INA.

The crucial point to note is that thanks to Subhas Bose's activities and the INA, the Armed Forces began to see themselves as defenders of India rather than upholders of the British Empire. This, more than anything else, was what led to India's freedom. This is also the reason why the British Empire disappeared from the face of the earth within an astonishingly short space of twenty years. Indian soldiers, who were the main prop of the Empire, were no longer willing to fight to hold the Empire together.

The story of India's freedom struggle, as it stands today is largely a political narrative and the contribution of the Indian soldiers has never been studied. Even today, the British look at the Indian army with a mixture of reverence and awe and say that had it not been for the Indian armed forces the outcome of the First and Second World War would have been totally different. They have a lot of anecdotes about the Indian army, which they had heard from their fathers, grandfathers and great grandfathers and they still remember and narrate them with a lot of fondness and respect for the Indian army.

The British government realised the danger of a revolt in a disgruntled army on whose loyalty depended the internal security of the country. During World War II when the Japanese armies were rapidly marching across Asia, their planes were bombing Calcutta (Kolkata) and Madras (Chennai) and the INA and Japanese brigades were ready to pounce on the Indo-Burmese border. The British realised the risk to the country. It was for this very purpose that the Cripps Mission (March-April 1942) was sent. Sir Stafford Cripps (a much-admired man in India) was sent to prevail upon the Indians to co-operate.

The British ruled the country with the help of the army, and this is the reason why they gave so much of importance to the army. A revolt by the armed forces would have been a catastrophe and a disaster for them. No country can get its freedom without bloodshed, so to think that the British left solely because of Gandhi's influence and activities is not only a mistake but a historical blunder. The British were scared of the army and not Gandhi. They could read the writing on the wall and their main reason for quitting the country was fear of mutiny by the Indian Armed Forces; particularly the army and activities of INA (Indian National Army) which were fresh in their minds.

And finally, The Sikh contribution in men and material during the two wars and also to the Indian National Army (INA), which played a very vital part in swaying the British Government's mind on the question of India's freedom, was the largest. A Sikh Captain (elevated to the rank of General by the Japanese) commanded the INA before Subhas Chander Bose.

The Role of Mahatama Gandhi

Gandhi helped cause India's independence from British rule, he did play his part and contribute his bit, but to give the whole sole credit of attaining freedom for the country to him would be a big fallacy. Some of his follies are enumerated:

The Jallianwala Bagh

On 13 April 1919, the **Jallianwala Bagh tragedy** took place, wherein the British officer, Brigadier General Dyer, ordered his forces to open fire on a peaceful gathering of innocent unarmed people. The official figures of the causalities were 379 killed and 1200 wounded, whereas the unofficial figures were much more. Gandhi forgave General Dyer (nicknamed the Butcher of Amritsar) again and again, even as he warned people against 'Dyerism' (a term coined by Gandhi to describe brute force and violent suppression). At that time Mahatma Gandhi was trying to show the country a different path – a path of non-violence and forgiveness. Gandhi even wrote that Dyer "merely destroyed a few bodies but the others tried to kill the soul of a nation." He said that "the fury that has been spent upon General Dyer is, I am sure, largely misdirected". (*Collected works of Mahatma Gandhi*, Volume 18, p.46, *Young India*, 14 July 1920). This was perhaps confusion of the mind and hypocrisy. For him everyone except he was a misguided patriot.

Khalifat Movement (1919 - 1924) and Moplah Rebellion or Agitation (1921 -22)

Since ages, every spring, just before the rains, when the winds turned eastwards, Arabian boats set sail to the Malabar Coast. The natives were use to their annual arrival as they were to the seasonal monsoon. They came to trade in dates and aromatic herbs (frankincense) and carry back Indian spices. The local population of Hindus welcomed them, some gave their daughters in marriage and allowed them to wed their women. Later, along with their merchandise they brought with them, their new faith (Islam). They built mosques and converted the inhabitants and early in the 9th century they gained a notable convert in the King of Malabar. As a result, few of these merchants stayed back and settled down in India. Gradually, colonies of Indo-Arab, Muslims grew along the west coast. They came to be known as *Mapilla*, meaning "great child" or "bridegroom/son-in-law" – the ancestors of the present day **Moplah** (Tara Chand, *Influence of Islam on Indian Culture*, p. 35).

The peaceful advent of Islam was suddenly checked when Muslim armies began to invade India. The Muslim incursions bred hatred in the minds of Hindus towards everything Muslim. As a result of the defeat of Turkey in the First World War, the influence of the Khalifa was immensely reduced. For all this the Indian Muslims held the English responsible and started the Khalifat Movement (1919 - 1924) against the British, to support and preserve the authority of the moribund Khilafat following the breakup of the Ottomon Empire, post-World War l, under the leadership of Maulana Shaukat Ali and Mohammed Ali. Gandhi realized that Hindus and Muslims must unite to fight the British and urged both the communities to show solidarity and unity. Consequently, the Khalifat Movement with doubtful ethical basis was taken up by Mr Gandhi with tenacity and faith as the Mahatma believed that by pleasing and supporting the Muslims, it would solidify Hindu-Muslim unity, instill an anti-British sentiment among Indian Muslims and then they could be easily drawn into an active political struggle against the British power. This measure had an adverse effect and in so doing Gandhi ended up feeding the hydra of Islamism in India.

The above-mentioned movement influenced, instigated and led up to the Malabar rebellion of 1921-22 (called Moplah rebellion or agitation, and also Mappila rebellion). It started as a resistance against the British colonial rule in Malabar region of Kerala. The popular uprising or agitation was also directed against the prevailing feudal system controlled by elite Hindus. The Khilafat had legitimised their conservative religious instincts and roused Muslim fears and suspicions about the outside world. It strengthened their communalism, which thrived on hatred against the Hindu *Kafirs* (non-believers) that was lying dormant. Essentially, the Khilafat Movement united Indian Muslims against non-believers or infidels, within India and outside and Gandhi's naive support to the movement only lent credence to the Moplah genocide of Hindus that followed. The Moplah Muslim community of Malabar had, for 100 years, indulged in bouts of murderous rage against heathens.

The genocide of Hindus in August-September 1921 was different because the Muslims thought they would oust the British and establish an Islamic State. The Hindus had to be massacred for it since *Kafirs* have no place in the "land of the pure". Officially, over 10,000 Hindus were slaughtered by Muslim fanatics. The unofficial numbers, likely far more accurate are much higher. In one such gruesome incident (25th of September 1921), on the barren hillside between Thuvoor and Karuvayakandi in North Kerala Chambrassery Imbichi Koithangal, 40 Hindus were caught hold of, their hands tied behind their backs and according to various accounts, 38 Hindus were charged with helping the military against the Moplah fanatics. These 38 were murdered, 3 of the 38 were shot but the rest were beheaded and thrown in the Thuvoor well.

The facts of the Moplah genocide of Hindus and the Khilafat movement are shamelessly concealed and whitewashed. However, the authentic accounts of the Moplah massacre/genocide that exist tell an incredible tale of forceful conversion, atrocities against Hindu men, women and even children and fanaticism that was aided by the support provided by Congress leaders, most prominently, MK Gandhi.

Hanging of Sardar Udam Singh and Bhagat Singh

Mahatma Gandhi could have averted the death sentence of Sardar Udham Singh and Sardar Bhagat Singh, but he put up a façade, displaying a pseudo sense of non-violence and peace and refused to intervene. The two gentlemen however, were prepared for death, perhaps they wanted to die and by their death they became more popular and immortal.

Race, Caste and Gandhi

Across the globe, the campaign to remove Gandhi's statues has become more and more common. Gandhi as a young man was "undoubtedly racist" and "showed very little interest in the afflictions of the black man." (Professor Ernest Aryeetey, University of Ghana). Groups calling themselves, Gandhi Must Fall in Ghana, Manchester (University of Manchester students in 2019) and students in Canada (2020) accuse Gandhi of being racist and say that removing Gandhi's statue was a "small step" towards addressing racism and discrimination. Today, Gandhi's racist past is linked to global anti-racist justice movements, like *Black Lives Matter*.

Gandhi's legacy is increasingly contested within India too as Hindu Nationalism gains currency and the possibilities of changing the constitution are also being considered. Among the vocal voices condemning Gandhi, calling him a betrayer, are members from the Hindu nationalist associations in India (views are by some members and not necessarily positions of the associations). Some of these people now glorify Godse and celebrate him as a patriot today, while blaming Gandhi for dividing the country and upholding anti-Hindu biases.

Gandhi's views on caste are also being challenged. Right-wing, upper caste Hindu ideologues feel that his constant appeals for piety and unity between various communities was the reason behind the partition at the time of India's independence, as well as the privileges religious minorities enjoyed in independent India. Gandhi saw untouchability as merely a social evil and believed that caste system should be integral to society. Endorsing the top and bottom castes in the hierarchy, he wrote: "The Brahmin's duty is to look after the sanitation of the soul, the *bhangi's* (sweeper's) that of the body of society". In contrast, Dr Ambedkar considered caste as integral to Hinduism and an anti-thesis of equality. Today, some accuse Gandhi of establishing a Brahmin rule in independent India.

As an Upper Caste leader, Gandhi began a fast 'onto death' in opposition to the Dalit leader Dr Bhimrao Ramji Ambedkar's demands for a separate electorate for India's marginalised communities belonging to the scheduled castes (SC) and only relented when Dr Ambedkar compromised vide the **Poona Pact of 1932**. **But it's notable that Gandhi did not object to similar provision for Muslims or Sikhs**. These decisions significantly shaped the fate of Dalit political representation in post-colonial India. The scheduled castes are averse to being counted as Hindus.

The Sikhs established the **Sarab Hind Sikh Mission** to lure Dr Bhimrao Ambedkar, preach against caste and propagate the Sikh Religion. Ambedkar did not join the Sikh faith, perhaps, for the reason that the Sikh religion does not have caste, but in practice caste exists. The Sikhs fought for schedule caste status for their downtrodden. The Constitution (Scheduled Castes) Order, 1950, under Article 341 stipulates that no person professing a religion different from Hinduism, Sikhism or Buddhism can be deemed to be a member of a Scheduled Caste. The original order under which only Hindus were classified as SCs was amended in 1956 to include Sikhs, and in 1990 to cover Buddhists.

As the ideals of equality and justice take centre stage in public discourse, Gandhi's views that supported inequality and injustice – even if they were early in his life and even if such support was implicit – will continue to be scrutinised in the times to come.

Role played by America

Another very important aspect is the role played by America and its Presidents in India's freedom. It must be remembered that United States of America got its freedom after fighting the British in the United States War of Independence or American Revolution (1775–83). In India all movements and agitations launched by Mahatma Gandhi had been suppressed ruthlessly by the British. In 1917, the British Prime Minister David Lloyd George approached the US President Woodrow Wilson for rendering help in the war effort during the First World War (1914–18). "What are we fighting for?" asked the US President. "For freedom of the free world," was the reply. "Then you should grant freedom to all the colonies under you at the end of the war," said President Woodrow Wilson. This was promised, but unfortunately at the end of the war in 1918, PM David Lloyd George conveniently forgot his promise.

During the Second World War (1939–45) precisely the same thing happened, only the faces had changed. But this time President Franklin Roosevelt took the pledge to free the colonies at the end of the war in writing from Mr Winston Churchill the then prime minister of England. Though Winston Churchill lost the election in 1945 at the end of World War II, the commitment was there in black and white. That was why the new prime minister Clement Attlee immediately declared in 1946 that India would get independence as early as possible. This became a reality in August 1947. An ungrateful nation should thank the United States of America and its presidents for facilitating its freedom.

9

ASSAULT ON THE GOLDEN TEMPLE BY THE INDIAN ARMY

05 JUNE 1984

THE INDIAN ARMY WENT INTO DARBAR SAHIB, AMRITSAR (GOLDEN TEMPLE COMPLEX) NOT TO ELIMINATE A POLITICAL FIGURE OR A POLITICAL MOVEMENT BUT TO SUPPRESS THE CULTURE OF A PEOPLE, TO ATTACK THEIR HEART, TO STRIKE A BLOW AT THEIR SPIRIT AND SELF CONFIDENCE.

(**JOYCE PETTIGREW, THE SIKHS OF PUNJAB**)
(LONDON: ZED PUBLISHERS, 1995)

The attack '**Operation Blue Star**' was wrongly conceived and timed (by design or default) because the day fixed for the assault was Guru Arjan's martyrdom day and pilgrims (including ladies and children) had gathered in large numbers for the religious ceremonies. Many of these devotees lost their lives. No accountability was given or responsibility taken.

This was the Third Ghallughara (Holocaust or Carnage)

The Indian army operation named '**Operation Blue Star**' (03-08 June 1984) managed to clear the Golden Temple.

Bhindranwale and his key lieutenants were killed.

Blue Star unleashed a cycle of revenge not seen since the partition of India and resulted in widespread mutiny of the Indian army's Sikh units.

On 31 October 1984 Indra Gandhi was assassinated.

During the Sikh pogrom of November 1984, eight thousand (three thousand in Delhi) Sikhs were systematically massacred. Official figures are 3,000.

The Indian government in power till May 2014 pretended that the Sikh pogrom of 1984 never happened.

Terrorism returned to Punjab and lasted a full decade till 1994. Twenty thousand (20,000) Sikhs were killed mostly in cold blood during insurgency in Punjab. The Official figures are 7,000.

Human rights organizations and newspapers across India believe the massacre was organized. It was a pogrom. The collusion of political officials, politicians and police in the massacre and the judiciary's failure to penalize the killers alienated normal Sikhs. Akal Takht, the governing religious body of Sikhs considers the killings to be **genocide**.

HOW CAN SUCH A THING BE FORGOTTEN, MUCH LESS FORGIVEN.

OPERATION BLUE STAR IS A SCAR TOO DEEP TO VANISH.

10

SIKH SACRIFICES

The Sikhs had to undergo, nearly two centuries of the worst state persecution and genocide, in human history; Sikh history is replete with examples of Sikh sacrifices. The fifth Guru of the Sikhs Guru Arjan was tortured to death when he asked for justice, liberty, equality and freedom of religion. Guru Hargobind, the sixth Guru was captured and incarcerated at Gwalior fort for six years for his growing popularity, martial preparations to protect human rights and religious freedom, and false allegations against him. Sixth Guru Har Krishan (boy Guru) succumbed to smallpox while tending to the sick and dying during an epidemic in Delhi. Tegh Bahadur, the ninth Guru, made the supreme sacrifice when he was beheaded in order to protect the right of the Hindus to wear their caste-marks and sacred threads. The tenth Guru Gobind Singh sacrificed all that he had for the freedom of the nation and the people – his parents, four sons, a large number of followers and ultimately himself.

Thousands of Sikhs died fighting or were caught and brutally massacred during the Mughal Rule and in various struggles, fights and wars thereafter. A broad mention of these events and incidents are:

- The four battles of Guru Hargobind when the Sikhs were forced to resort to arms.

- Battles of Guru Gobind Singh

- Battles of Banda Singh Bahadur
- Persecution of Sikhs by Mughals after Banda's death
- The two *Ghallugharas* (Holocausts or Carnages)
- Conducting guerrilla warfare and fighting battles (against Afghans and Mughals) during the *Misl* (Sikh confederacy) and Dal Khalsa (Sikh army) period
- During battles of Khalsa Raj (rule) i.e., Maharaja Ranjit Singh's rule
- Clashes, confrontations, happenings, and occurrences in the period of turmoil after the Maharaja's death
- The two Anglo-Sikh Wars
- Persecution by the British
- 1857 Mutiny
- Jallianwala Bagh incident
- World Wars I and II
- Revolts, agitations and clashes (including Gurdwara Movement) during fight for independence
- Riots and exodus during partition
- Three Indo-Pak wars (1947, !965, 1971) and the Kargil war, and also the 1962 Sino-Indian (Indo-China) war and various boarder conflicts and clashes

- The Third Ghallughara viz. Operation Blue Star and Sikh pogrom, and insurgency before and after this

- Various agitations, *hartals* (general strike), *bandhs* (meaning close i.e., stop work by closing all public offices, shops, schools etc.), *morchas* (battle front/entrenchment/hostile demonstration) and demonstrations for Punjabi *suba* (state), Punjabi language, Mandal commission etc. in independent/free India

During the Freedom struggle out of 2,175 patriots who gave their lives for the country's freedom, 1,557 were Sikhs, out of 2,646 sentenced to Andaman Island (Kala Pani) for life imprisonment, 2,147 (81%) were Sikhs, out of 127 martyrs who were hanged, 92 (71%) were Sikhs, out of 1,202 people shot at Jallianwala Bagh, 799 (61%) were Sikhs and out of 42000 soldiers, who served in INA (Indian National Army/Azad Hind Fauj) 28000 (67%) were Sikhs. The representation in of the Sikhs everywhere has far exceeded their strength in numbers. And, yet when they ask for their rights and promises made to them, they are dubbed as terrorists and Khalistanis, and they are reminded time and again that they are a minority and can take their due share as per their strength in numbers.

And yet how many people in the cow belt call Sikhs lackeys of the British; between UP and Bihar are the least number exiled and sent to the Andamans or hanged and yet they form the maximum number of freedom fighters drawing pension since 1947!!

Colossal amount of money has been spent and hundreds of thousands of precious Sikh lives have perished from the earth. But what have the Sikhs gained? Where is the Anandpur Sahib Resolution – the document that was the talk of the town during

Sikh insurgency? And, hundreds of more questions can be asked. The Sikh *netas* (leaders and politicians) are making a fool of the Sikh masses and the naïve and gullible Sikhs are playing into their hands. They (the leaders) want to be in power and make money at any cost even if they have to get their own people killed. It is all about money and power. They do not want competition and the major competitors must be eliminated.

The politicians in the state and center will never let the Khalistan issue die because it suits them and will garner votes. Sikhs must realise that it is only a small clique that rules and not everybody. It is high time the Sikhs woke up to the situation and gave this hated, shameless and corrupt scum a royal boot. If these people just possessed an inkling of an iota of their sublime and noble religion, they would not be swindling the poor innocent folk. Sikh theology principles are direct, clear and rock solid though an interminable gulf separates principle from practice.

The Sikh leaders being guided by fear (insecurity) and greed must realize that in a welfare and democratic state they are public servants and their job is serving the people and not looting them. Governments are there not to rule people but to serve (look after) them. They must apprehend that an innovative and honest person cannot really generate wealth for himself on a satisfactory and sustainable basis unless he works out a way to make his community wealthy as well. When the people around these corrupt leaders are earning enough, then these *netas* will automatically start generating abundance of wealth. This is the way to make money and grow opulent, happily and not corruption and dishonesty. These are bad and testing times, if things don't improve catastrophe is guaranteed, weirdly it is promised. The politicians have promised that they will not mend their ways and the public is in deep slumber.

Sikh survival, wellbeing, strength, prosperity and progress lies in education, unity, management of resources, economic empowerment, keeping alive their glorious history and faith, tolerance, harmony and peaceful co-existence as taught by their noble, sublime, humanitarian and cosmic religion. There is nothing that they lack, it is only rampant corruption that is gnawing at their entrails and refusal to learn from past mistakes. Why can't they educate themselves from the small Jain and Parse communities of India?

Every country has the government it deserves.
- Joseph DE Maistre, Letter, August 1811

BIBLIOGRAPHY

1. History of the Sikhs and their Religion (Three Volumes) – Edited by Kirpal Singh and Kharak Singh (published by SGPC)

2. The Encyclopedia of Sikhism (Four Volumes) – Harbans Singh (Editor-in Chief)

3. The Sikh Religion (Six Volumes) – M. A. Macauliffe

4. A History of the Sikhs (Two Volumes) – Khushwant Singh

5. The Sikhs Today – Khushwant Singh

6. Evolution of the Khalsa (Two Volumes) – Indubhusan Banerjee

7. The Sikhs and their Scriptures – C. H. Loehlin

8. A Brief Account of the Sikh People – Teja Singh and Ganda Singh

9. Life of Banda Singh Bahadur – Ganda Singh

10. Ranjit Singh – Sir Lapel Griffin, K. C. S. I.

11. The Court and Camp of Ranjeet Singh – W. G. Osborne

12. The Great Divide – H. V. Hodson

13. Fragments of Half a Century – Karnail Singh

14. The Sikh People Yesterday and Today – K. S. Duggal

15. Robber noblemen – Joyce Pettigrew

16. Fighting for Faith and Nation – Cynthia Keppley Mahmood

17. History of The Punjab Class XII (Punjab) – Professor Manjeet Singh Sodhi

18. Issues of Abstracts of Sikh Studies

19. Issues of Sikh Review

20. Encyclopedia Britannica

21. History of India (1000-1707A.D.) – A. L. Srivastava

22. History of India – D. N. Kundra and S. D. Kundra

23. Internet (Wikipedia, the free encyclopedia)

www.ingramcontent.com/pod-product-compliance
Lightning Source LLC
Chambersburg PA
CBHW062105160726
48282CB00026B/679
* 9 7 8 9 3 9 5 7 7 3 3 0 0 *